D0968820

TEACHING PLATO IN PALESTINE

TEACHING PLATO IN PALESTINE

PHILOSOPHY IN A DIVIDED WORLD

CARLOS FRAENKEL

PRINCETON UNIVERSITY PRESS

PRINCETON AND OXFORD

Published by Princeton University Press, 41 William Street,
Princeton, New Jersey 08540
In the United Kingdom: Princeton University Press, 6 Oxford Street,
Woodstock, Oxfordshire OX20 1TW
press.princeton.edu

Jacket photograph © Galyna Andrushko/Shutterstock.
Jacket design by Leslie Flis

Portions of Chapter 1 originally appeared as "Teaching Plato in Palestine," *Dissent* 54, no. 2 (Spring 2007): 32–39. Portions of Chapter 2 originally appeared as "Teaching Aristotle in Indonesia," *Dissent* 55, no. 3 (Summer 2008): 5–13. Published by the University of Pennsylvania Press.

ISBN 978-0-691-15103-8

Library of Congress Control Number: 2014956072

British Library Cataloging-in-Publication Data is available

This book has been composed in Linux Libertine

Printed on acid-free paper. ∞

Printed in the United States of America

1 3 5 7 9 10 8 6 4 2

For Lara and Ben
and in memory of
Joaquim Câmara Ferreira

CONTENTS

FOREWORD

Michael Walzer

Carlos Fraenkel is a talented philosopher and historian of philosophy who is also interested, as most contemporary philosophers are not, in theological arguments. His most recent book, *Philosophical Religions from Plato to Spinoza: Reason, Religion, and Autonomy*, is an innovative addition to an academic literature that is often short on innovation. But Fraenkel has interests that reach far beyond academic literature. He actually believes that philosophy can be useful to the lay public, to people like you and me, who are not professional philosophers, who argue in ordinary language about God, the moral law, the best political regime, the possibility of true knowledge, and how one should live.

I think of Fraenkel as a philosophical adventurer who "does philosophy" in strange places, far from its familiar academic haunts. It all started with "Teaching Plato in Palestine," the book's first chapter, originally an article in *Dissent* magazine (I was then the coeditor). What an idea this was, and so beautifully executed and described—to discuss classical and medieval philosophy with young Palestinians who were also devout Muslims. Of course, there once were great Muslim Platonists and Aristotelians, who developed philosophical systems of their own and transmitted Greek knowledge to Jews and Christians. But the recent religious revivals in Islam, and in Judaism and Christianity too, have not been much attuned to classical, or any other, philosophy. Nor have they been open to the kind of discussions that Fraenkel wanted to have, and did have, with his students. His aim in East Jerusalem, and then in his later adventures with Indonesian Muslims, Hasidic Jews, Brazilian teenagers, and members of an Iroquois community in Canada, was to use philosophical tools to engage the questions that people in these places are grappling with—and this without shying away from disagreements. On the contrary: we should welcome disagreements, Fraenkel argues, and make them fruitful for what he calls a "culture of debate." How to do it? How do you argue about the hardest questions with reason and logic and respect for all the counterarguments?

"Teaching Plato in Palestine" was grist for *Dissent*'s mill, and Fraenkel also gave us the Indonesia piece that became the book's second chapter. We are committed not only to debate but also to our own version of Fraenkel's fallibilism that he outlines in the second part of the book: we worry incessantly about our own positions and commitments. This book is an argument that everyone should do that, and it will go some way toward making fallibilism, which has never been one of the popular "isms," into a comprehensible and attractive creed. Oliver Cromwell once told a group of Presbyterian ministers, "Think ye in the bowels of Christ, that ye may be wrong!" Wherever you think, Fraenkel wants you to contemplate your possible wrongness. But he also wants all of us to defend what we believe and to engage with others who believe differently—and to make philosophy the tool of the defense and the engagement.

He doesn't like the version of multiculturalism that has people sitting, so to speak, all in their own individual neighborhoods, practicing their own religion or culture, safe among themselves only because they are radically disengaged from everyone else. There is a better, more humane, and more productive safety, he insists, among people who learn to converse and discuss across cultural and religious boundaries. Fraenkel aspires to an Athens where the people don't kill Socrates but imitate him—and then answer each other's questions. He insists that this Athens isn't a utopia. It's a real place—in East Jerusalem, Makassar, and Brooklyn, in Brazil and Canada, where people meet and argue. Now listen to his account of those arguments.

PREFACE

In 2000, I was working on Arabic and Hebrew philosophical texts for my doctoral thesis and decided to spend a few months in Cairo to brush up on my Arabic. Once settled in, I organized a language exchange with Egyptian students. As we got to know each other better, we also became concerned about each other's way of life. They wanted to save my soul from eternally burning in hell by converting me to Islam. I wanted to save them from wasting their real life for an illusory afterlife by converting them to the secular worldview I grew up with. "Betting on Islam," one student, Muhammad, argued, "gets you a three-in-one deal, because Muslims also believe in the God of Jews and Christians." "But I don't believe in God at all," I replied. "So are you sure that we can't prove God's existence?" Muhammad asked. The question took me by surprise. Where I had been intellectually socialized, this was taken for granted. I tried to reproduce Kant's critique of the ontological proof of God. "Fine," Muhammad said, "but what about this table, does its existence depend on a cause?" "Of course," I answered. "And its cause depends on a further cause?" Muhammad was referring to the metaphysical proof of God's existence, formulated by the Muslim philosopher Avicenna in the eleventh century: since an infinite regress of causes is impossible, Avicenna argues, things that depend on a cause for their existence must have something that exists through itself as their first cause. And this necessary existent is God.[1] I had a counterargument to that, to which they, in turn, had a rejoinder. The discussion ended inconclusively.

I did not convert to Islam, nor did my Egyptian friends become atheists. But experiences such as this gave rise to the two main questions I grapple with in this book: Can doing philosophy be useful outside the confines of academia? And can philosophy help turn tensions that arise from diversity (cultural, religious, and so forth) into what I propose calling a "culture of debate"? On both counts, I argue, we should be optimistic. In the first and main part of the book I make a practical case for taking philosophy out of the classroom. In the second part I sketch arguments for a culture of debate.

The practical case is based on five philosophy workshops that I organized between 2006 and 2011: at a Palestinian university in East Jerusalem, at an Islamic university in Indonesia, with members of Hasidic communities in New York, with high school students in Salvador da Bahia, the center of Afro-Brazilian culture, and in a Mohawk Indigenous community in North America. I chose the locations deliberately along various lines of conflict: Israel and Palestine, Islam and the West, religious orthodoxy and modernity, social and racial divisions in Brazil, and the struggle of Indigenous nations with the legacy of colonialism. These conflicts give rise to fundamental questions on topics ranging from metaphysics and religion to morality and politics: Does God exist? Is piety worth it? Can violence be justified? What is social justice, and how can we get there? Who should rule? What does political self-determination require? Such questions affected my students at multiple levels—from their individual beliefs to the values held by small groups, like the Hasidic communities in New York, to the future direction of entire nations, as in Indonesia and Brazil. Philosophy, I argue, can help to articulate these questions more clearly, and to explore and refine answers to them.

One thing my interlocutors around the world had in common was strong religious or cultural commitments that often clashed with my secular views. As in my discussions with Egyptian students, I often realized that I hadn't properly thought through some of the most basic convictions that constitute my worldview: from my atheism to my beliefs about how one should live. I was forced to think hard about these convictions that normally aren't questioned in the Western academic milieu I come from. The workshops thus gave me firsthand insight into how divided we are on moral, religious, and philosophical issues. In the book's second part I argue that, although many people find these disagreements disheartening, they can be a good thing—if we succeed in transforming them into a culture of debate. Conceived as a joint search for the truth, a culture of debate gives us a chance to examine the beliefs and values we were brought up with and often take for granted. It is more attractive than either forcing our views on others or becoming mired in multicultural complacency—as if differences didn't matter at all. Here, too, I contend, philosophy can take on an important role: providing the foundation for a culture of debate.

By "philosophy" I don't mean a particular philosophical worldview (for example, Marxism or existentialism). What I mean is the *practice* of philosophy: acquiring *techniques of debate*—logical and semantic tools that allow us to clarify our views and to make and respond to arguments (a contemporary version of what Aristotelians called the *Organon*, the "tool kit" of the philosopher)—and cultivating *virtues of debate*—valuing the truth more than winning an argument and trying one's best to understand the viewpoint of the opponent. A culture of debate, in other words, is based not on the sophistical skill of making one's own opinion prevail over others, but on the dialectical skill of engaging in a joint search for the truth. In the workshops, we also discussed the works of philosophers from Plato to Nietzsche that provided both a starting point for the discussion and sufficient distance from immediate concerns. As much as possible, these included texts with ties to the workshops' cultural settings—for example, medieval Muslim and Jewish philosophers—with the aim to build on local traditions of debate and reflection.

Let me add three further clarifications. First, my aim is not to question the value of academic philosophy and its patient and technically sophisticated pursuit of clarity. I am myself thoroughly engaged in the discipline and enjoy discussion with graduate students and writing for a specialized audience. At the same time, I believe that the value of philosophy is *not limited* to its academic practice and that it is possible and enriching to move back and forth between the two spheres. Second, this is not a secular project where philosophy aims to usurp the guiding role of religion. I already mentioned that most of my interlocutors were deeply religious. As my discussion with students in Egypt illustrates, and as I argue in some detail in the book's second part, the practice of philosophy can cut across cultural boundaries, including the secular-religious divide. Third, this is not at all about a great philosopher descending to the level of ordinary citizens to share his wisdom with them. On the contrary: through the discussions I realized how narrow even my repertoire of questions was. In this sense I greatly benefited from the opportunity to puzzle about issues that wouldn't have come up in my normal academic life. The idea, then, is not to give philosophers a say about what we should think and do, but to enable as many people as possible to acquire the practice of philosophy. And here I think academic philosophers can contribute something after many years of training: by sharing the tools that can help us to think through questions related to ourselves, our communities, and the world we live in—no matter which answers we ultimately settle on.

I did not choose the locations of the workshops only because they were helpful for thinking about the questions I am interested in. They are also tied to my biography and scholarly expertise. This gave me some linguistic and cultural competence to moderate the discussions, and allowed me to add a personal angle to the narrative. Throughout the book I maintain a conversational tone to engage nonspecialist readers. This is especially the case for the essays of the first part, which can also be read as a kind of intellectual travelogue. Although the second part presents a more systematic argument, it doesn't presuppose technical philosophical knowledge. There I also intervene in a debate that has been central to political philosophy since early modern times: how to approach diversity and disagreement. My hope is that, on the whole, the book shows by example and argument that making philosophy part of our personal and public lives is something worthwhile.

PART I

TEACHING PLATO IN PALESTINE

Can philosophy save the Middle East? It can. This, at least, is the thesis of Sari Nusseibeh as I learn from a friend upon arriving in Israel in February 2006. Nusseibeh is not only a prominent Palestinian intellectual and the Palestinian Liberation Organization's former chief representative in Jerusalem, but also a philosopher by training (and, I think, by nature, too). "*Only* philosophy," the friend tells me he argued during the Shlomo Pines memorial lecture in West Jerusalem three years before (aptly titled "On the Relevance of Philosophy in the Arab World Today"). By the time I leave Israel, I'm convinced that he's on to something.

I am here to teach a seminar at Al-Quds University, the Palestinian university in Jerusalem, together with Nusseibeh, who has been president of Al-Quds since 1995. My idea is to discuss Plato's political thought with the students and then examine how medieval Muslim and Jewish philosophers built on this thought to interpret Islam and Judaism as philosophical religions. I hope to raise some basic questions about philosophy and its relationship to politics and religion, and also to open a new perspective on the contemporary Middle East.

The texts, I suspect, will resonate quite differently with my Palestinian students than they do with my students in Montreal. Unfortunately, the available Arabic translations of Plato are based on Benjamin Jowett's nineteenth-century English version, itself more a paraphrase than an accurate rendering, which translators sometimes painfully butcher. No doubt, in this respect, things have changed for the worse since the Middle Ages. From the eighth century to the tenth, excellent translations were made of Greek scientific and philosophical texts. It was an impressive achievement: one civilization appropriated the knowledge of another and turned it into the basis of its own vibrant intellectual culture. This, moreover, was not the project of some isolated intellectuals; it was a large-scale enterprise carried out under the patronage of the political, social, and economic elite of the Abbasid caliphate (the second Sunni dynasty that ruled the Muslim empire; it seized power from the Umayyads in 750).[1] After the Greeks, the next significant period in the history of philosophy and science thus unfolded within Islamic civilization. Its main intellectual centers were Baghdad, the residence of the Abbasid caliphs, and al-Andalus (Muslim Spain), the last stronghold of the Umayyads.

I arrive in Jerusalem with the course syllabus, the texts, and an introductory lecture. After a few failed attempts to contact "Doctor Sari" (as Nusseibeh is called here), I decide to simply show up at his office in East Jerusalem.

How well, I wonder, is my classroom *fuṣḥā*—the high Arabic of the Quran, the media, and literature that nobody actually speaks—going to work in the street? "Can you tell me where Al-Quds University is?" I venture to ask two passing girls. At first they look puzzled, then they giggle. "You mean Al-Uds University, right?" (The Palestinian dialect, like the Egyptian, almost always drops the "q.") At the administrative office of "Al-Uds" University I drink a coffee with Hanan, Sari Nusseibeh's secretary. It turns out that Doctor Sari is traveling in India and Pakistan and will be back only for the second week of classes. "So I'll have to teach the first class alone?" I ask, a little surprised and a little worried. "I'm afraid yes," Hanan answers. Then she prints out the information about philosophy seminar 0409438, to be taught by "Doctor Sari and Doctor Carlos."

I choose to live in Rehavia, one of the oldest quarters in Jewish Jerusalem, known as the quarter of the professors because many European academics and intellectuals (Martin Buber, Shlomo Pines, and Gershom Scholem, among others) settled here—scholars "with a worldwide reputation," as Israeli writer Amos Oz recalls his father whispering into his ear every time they spotted one on their walks through the neighborhood. "I thought that having a worldwide reputation was somehow related to having weak legs," writes Oz in his memoir, "because the person in question was often an elderly man who felt his way with a stick and stumbled as he walked along."[2] Although as of yet I have neither a stick nor a worldwide reputation, I'm again renting an apartment here, having already spent three years in the neighborhood as a graduate student, each of them living on a different street: Ibn Ezra, Ben Maimon, and Alfasi. The streets in Rehavia are named after prominent Jewish scholars of another time and place: medieval thinkers whose intellectual world was decisively shaped by Islamic civilization.

The street called Rehov ben Maimon is named after Maimonides, whom many consider to be the greatest Jewish philosopher. Like Averroes, his equally famous Muslim colleague, Maimonides was born in twelfth-century Córdoba, which two centuries before had been the most sophisticated place in Europe. Maimonides and Averroes received the same philosophical-scientific education and became the last two major representatives of Arabic philosophy in medieval Spain. Averroes interpreted Islam as a philosophical religion; Maimonides did the same for Judaism. They are religions founded by philosopher-prophets that not only form the moral character of those who live according to their laws, but also direct them to the intellectual love of God—to physics, the study of God's wisdom in nature, and to metaphysics, the study of God's attributes.[3] Maimonides wrote his philosophical works in Arabic, the idiom of science and philosophy of his time. In the instructions he left to a student about which philosophical works are worth studying, he recommends not a single Jewish author. After the Greeks, in particular Aristotle and his commentators, the philosophers he praises are all Muslims: al-Fārābī (d. ca. 950), who "excelled in wisdom," for example, and Ibn Bājja (d. 1138), whose "treatises are all good for the person who understands."[4] Of course Maimonides does not praise them because they are Muslims, but because they are good philosophers. "One must," he claims, "listen to *al-Ḥaqq* from whoever says it."[5] (*Al-Ḥaqq* means "the truth" in Arabic; it is also one of God's names.) If someone proposes a definition of an animal species, explains the meaning of justice, or works out a proof for God's existence, what matters is not whether he is Jewish, Muslim, Christian or something else, but whether what he says is true.

This is an idea I also later discuss with the five young men and three young women who signed up for the class. Does philosophy provide a language with which people can communicate even if they do not accept each other's religious commitments? Can we say that they are able to do so because as rational beings they can understand and evaluate an argument without regard to the background of the one who makes it? After some debate, most of the students agree that this seems no less valid now than it was at the time of Maimonides and Averroes. They also point to a genre of apologetic literature widespread in the Islamic world today: books that through interpretation locate modern scientific insights in verses of the Quran without regard to the scientist's background. "Can you give me an example?" I ask. "For example, the theory of relativity," Ahmed answers. Einstein, I remind them, was Jewish and had been offered the presidency of Israel.

It is interesting to note in this context that Nusseibeh himself taught Islamic philosophy at the Hebrew University in 1979–80. Promoting collaboration with Israeli universities is important to him. In reaction to the boycott of Israeli academic institutions declared by the British Association of University Teachers in 2005, Nusseibeh signed a joint statement with Menachem Magidor, the president of the Hebrew University, in which they "insist on continuing to work together in the pursuit of knowledge."[6] On the Palestinian side, this stance meets with little appreciation. A week before I leave, Nusseibeh tells me about a declaration by the Palestinian Union of University Teachers that he should be dismissed from Al-Quds for "normalizing ties with Israel" and "serving Israeli propaganda interests." "The next thing," he tells me, "is that they will put me on trial." It's not the first attempt to ostracize him. Among the more absurd rumors I hear on campus is that he maintains his position only because the Israeli Security Service, the Shin Bet, protects him. (In 1991, in fact, he was briefly jailed by the Shin Bet for allegedly telling the Iraqi ambassador to Tunisia on the phone where in Israel Saddam Hussein's Scud missiles landed!)[7]

The controversy about Nusseibeh's commitment to speaking with the "enemy" is old. In 1987, he was severely beaten after helping to arrange the first meeting between PLO members and members of Israel's right-wing Likud. The masked aggressors belonged to his own political party, the Fataḥ faction of the PLO. The beating occurred on the campus of Birzeit University, near Ramallah, where he was a professor of philosophy, after a lecture on John Locke, liberalism, and tolerance.[8] (So it's not surprising that I never see him without his bodyguards. They inspect the classroom before he comes in and guard the door during class.) The controversy reached a climax after Nusseibeh claimed in an article ("What Next?") that "all rational people" in the region must admit that peace can be achieved only under three conditions: that Israel withdraws to the 1967 borders, that Palestinians concede the right to return to Israel, and that both sides agree on a shared government of Jerusalem.[9] This position underlies a further joint effort: the proposal for a resolution of the Israeli-Palestinian conflict that he signed in 2002 with Ami Ayalon, the former head of the Shin Bet.[10] Saying in public that reason demands that the land be shared made Nusseibeh (whose mother's family lost everything in the 1948 war) a traitor in the eyes of many Palestinians.[11]

My first class is scheduled for the same Saturday as the first session of the new Palestinian Parliament, in which Hamas has an absolute majority (a most unwelcome surprise for Israel and the West, although a legitimate democratic decision). In the end the Parliament convenes, but the class is cancelled. Al-Quds University is on strike because salaries have not been paid. For now the more basic needs of material life have halted the dissemination of wisdom.

I try to set up a first meeting with Nusseibeh, who has returned from his travels to mediate the strike. I call his secretary, who informs me that he's in a meeting and gives me the number of his assistant, who likewise informs me that he's in a meeting and gives me the number of another assistant, who again informs me that he's in a meeting. But it pays to be persistent. The secretary calls me back; we arrange (what else?) a meeting at Nusseibeh's office. He holds lots of meetings. The administration of the university is not a light burden; it does not leave much time for philosophy. "But I've found ways to integrate the two," he explains, "by analyzing philosophically the problems I encounter every day." Administering Al-Quds under the present circumstances is a permanent exercise in practical reasoning. "Nothing is predictable," he says. That's the challenge that keeps him going. "If things would work just fine I'd be happy to go back to a life of contemplation." It makes him a bit jealous when I tell him that I'm sometimes bored with too much time for contemplation in peaceful Montreal. But he hasn't given up on inquiring into God and nature. At age fifty-seven, he says, "I do want to understand for myself how it all hangs together before the end."

During the meeting (and also later in class) the prayer beads of a *subḥa* run through his fingers—not, I think, because he's reciting *al-asmāʾ al-ḥusnā* (the "Beautiful Names," or ninety-nine names of God). It looks more like a way to relieve tension, like the cigarettes he chain-smokes. He remains silent while his son, Absal, and Huda Imam, the director of the Center for Jerusalem Studies, relate in detail how, on the way back to Jerusalem from a poetry reading in Ramallah, they were interrogated for hours by Israeli soldiers. Despite Nusseibeh's silence, the complaints about Israeli soldiers' behavior at roadblocks are a recurring theme throughout my stay. For the Palestinians this is a particularly painful experience of the imbalance of power. (More than half of the students miss the class after Israel's Independence Day. Because it is the most symbolic time for attacks, control is correspondingly tight.)

A week later the strike ends and classes begin. Getting to the campus at Abu Dis, a suburb of East Jerusalem, turns out to be a challenge in itself. (Al-Quds also has a campus in the Old City; the problem is that Israel doesn't let the students from the territories cross the border.) It's only ten minutes away from the center of East Jerusalem, but now you need to take two taxis to get there: the first brings you as far as *al-jidār*, the controversial separation wall Israel is building. A massive, nearly five-meter-high piece of this construction suddenly grows out of the street. Nasr, an employee of the university's administration, shows me how to climb over a neighboring garden wall to the other side of *al-jidār*. We wait for a moment while a group coming the opposite way makes it safely to our side. When it's our turn, I'm warned to be careful. (Rehavia scholars with weak legs and worldwide reputations would run into difficulties here, I'm afraid.) From there, a second taxi takes you to the university.

At our first class meeting I don't get very far with my prepared introduction. After a couple of sentences, Nusseibeh interrupts me, asks critical questions, and presents arguments for the contrary position. The students are confused—precisely the effect he's intended. He aims to get them thinking, not just writing down Dr. Carlos's words of wisdom, and there's no better way to achieve that than by having two professors disagree in the classroom.

Nusseibeh likes to challenge the students' intellectual habits. During the semester visiting lectures are presented by several top scholars and artists, such as Joseph Raz, a leading philosopher of law, and theater director Peter Brook, who brings in his troupe from the Bouffes du Nord theater in Paris to stage a South African play—half comedy, half tragedy—about life under apartheid. "Ideally I would like to see the students travel and discover the world for themselves," Nusseibeh tells me, "spend a month in Florence, learning Italian, visiting art galleries and monuments, and reading Italian literature." But these students cannot even get to Jerusalem or Gaza. So he tries his best to bring the world to Abu Dis.

At first view, much here seems adverse to a life of contemplation. I wonder, though, if the permanent state of collision, affecting all aspects of life, might not ignite philosophical inquiry into concepts like justice, rights, power, and so forth. Couldn't clarifying these concepts help navigate the conflict and move toward a solution? I left Jerusalem after completing my doctorate in 2000, shortly before Arafat, Barak, and Clinton met at Camp David. Back then there was real optimism; the solution of the conflict seemed possible—it was actually poised to happen. In the end, distrust prevailed. Now, in order to eat lunch at the Hebrew University, I have to pass a fourfold control: at the entrance to the university a guard inspects the bus looking for suspicious passengers; after I leave the bus, another guard checks my passport and the letter attesting that I'm a visiting scholar; next my bag is examined and I'm given an electronic body check; finally my bag is examined again at the entrance to the student restaurant. About five young security officers participate in the procedures. At my last visit, more than three years ago, only one old man briefly looked at the bag and asked, "Are you armed?"

The first text we look at is Plato's *Apology*, discussing Socrates's claim that "it is the greatest good for man to talk about virtue every day and those other things about which you hear me testing myself and others; for the unexamined life is not worth living."[12] (Even Socrates's excitement about the afterlife stems from the opportunity it will offer to "examine" the great poets and heroes of the Greek past!)[13] Socrates's idea of a good time sounds as strange to my Palestinian students as it does to my students in Montreal. What does Socrates mean by the "examined life," and why is it so important? I suggest to them that in Socrates's view living a virtuous life depends on grounding one's life on knowledge. In order to act justly, for example, you must understand justice. "Why can't we rely on the notion of justice transmitted by religion?" Shirin, one of the students, asks. "Can you be sure that this notion is correct without examining it?" I ask in reply. We go through some standard examples from the Israeli-Palestinian conflict, where things were done that the agents claimed to be just and religiously motivated, but whose justice is obviously doubtful: from Baruch Goldstein's 1994 massacre of Palestinians in Hebron and the assassination of Yitzhak Rabin by Yigal Amir in 1995, to the 2002 suicide bombing at Rehavia's Café Moment where I'd often gone for dinner or drinks as a graduate student.

To illustrate what may have led someone like Socrates to question traditional moral norms, I recount a friend's description of the beginning of her philosophical quest. She was born into a Jewish family in Jerusalem. Her father worked full-time, and when she was three months old, her mother returned to her work as a flight attendant. With her mother gone for days, she mostly grew up with a Muslim Palestinian nanny. She became fluent in Arabic, called her nanny "mother," and spent much of her childhood with the nanny's family. As a consequence, she experienced the conflict between Israelis and Palestinians from both perspectives: the often humiliating treatment of Arabs in Israel, for example, and the pain and anger when one of her aunts was killed on a bus by a Palestinian suicide bomber. Growing up between two narratives that contradict each other led to confusion, and confusion led to the wish to find out for herself what is right and wrong. This, she told me, got her into philosophy.

There was plenty of confusion about right and wrong in Socrates's time. I mention Herodotus's account of how Greeks began to question their customs after encountering other cultures. These customs, they realized, may not be universally valid norms. A funeral ritual considered pious in Greece, for example, was considered an abomination in India, and vice versa.[14] Hence, the Socratic question, what really is piety? But note that this is not about opposing knowledge to religious tradition. Socrates only wants you to make sure that your teachers or preachers told you the truth when they explained the meaning of piety, justice, and other such things.

Although most of the students accept the idea that it is important to examine religious notions in a Socratic manner, their commitment to the truth of Islam leaves no room for confusion. During the discussion, Hassan turns the question around: "How can a secular citizen of a liberal Western democracy live an examined life?" Religious Muslims feel the need to justify the life they choose and to explain why it is superior to that of others. Citizens in the West, on the other hand, experience neither confusion nor the need to seek, like Socrates, objective standards. They often take freedom to mean that each individual chooses how to live according to personal preferences and see all choices as equal. "You're right," I reply, "this kind of relativism makes examination futile. But isn't it the same if you take the truth of Islam for granted?" Perhaps not. I point out that there's much division in Islam. "So even if Islam were true, don't you have to examine its many different interpretations?" I ask. Bilal mentions a famous hadith in which the Prophet Muhammad predicts that the *ummah* (the Muslim community) will split into seventy-three sects. "And only one goes to heaven!" "Which one is it?" I ask. "The Sunnis of course," he replies. All the students are mainstream Sunnis, the largest Muslim denomination. "Don't Shīʿites also claim that they're the only ones who will be saved?" I press on. "Yes, but they're wrong!" Amreen counters. "How can you be so sure? If you had been born into a Shīʿite family in Iran, wouldn't you say the same thing about Sunnis?" She points out that about 80 percent of Muslims are Sunnis. "But is truth a matter of the greatest number? Can't the majority be wrong?" I ask.

After class, Nusseibeh usually gives me a ride back from Abu Dis to Jerusalem. We talk about many things. On one occasion, he tells me that his British wife, Lucy, is sometimes more fond than he is of living in Palestine. She is the daughter of the Oxford philosopher John L. Austin, author of an analytical philosophy classic: *How to Do Things with Words.* Nusseibeh and Lucy met at Oxford, where he earned his undergraduate degree in philosophy, before completing his doctorate at Harvard with a thesis on the metaphysics of the medieval Islamic philosopher Avicenna. After her undergraduate years at Oxford, Lucy converted to Islam, married Nusseibeh, and became a leading activist for peace and nonviolence in Palestine.

On another occasion we discuss education and democracy. How many books could have been translated from Arabic and into Arabic with the hundreds of billions of dollars that the United States put into the Iraq War? Surely we would have reliable translations of Plato to work with. How many exchange and scholarship programs between Western and Arab schools and universities could have been established? For anyone who is serious about democracy in the Middle East, isn't this the way to go?

The example of the Iraq War seems to make one thing clear: democracy cannot easily be imposed from the outside. Of course, democracy doesn't depend only on sharing knowledge. Israel's occupation can't be overlooked, and there are plenty of despots in the region who need to be chased away.[15] But to the extent that democracy means self-determination on the basis of informed choices, developing tools for choosing and sharing information about available options seems the right thing. The key is knowledge and how to use it.

I am not talking about one civilization "educating" another. One suggestion I make in class is that the West and the Muslim world have enough shared traditions to conduct an open discussion on an equal footing. After all, the intellectual configurations of both were largely shaped by the encounter of monotheistic religion and Greek philosophy and science.

But the dialogue doesn't have to be with the West in the first place. Intellectual resources within Islam abound that allow it to engage in a debate with itself. It's mostly a question of going beyond the monolithic interpretation proposed by Islamic fundamentalists to rediscover the wide variety of positions that were defended in the history of Islamic thought. They range from that of Abū Bakr al-Rāzī (d. 925) to that of Ibn Taymiyya (d. 1328). Al-Rāzī, who refers to Socrates as "my Imām" in his philosophical autobiography, rejected the authority of revealed religion almost a thousand years before Voltaire, arguing that God provided all human beings with reason sufficient to guide them in life. So there's no need for additional guidance by prophets.[16] Ibn Taymiyya, at the other end of the spectrum, not only rejected certain philosophical positions as incompatible with religion, but attacked even the use of logic as a Greek adulteration of pure Islam.[17] And there are many intermediate positions, one of which we later take up in class: the integration of religion into a rationalist framework.

In today's Arab world, Palestine has one of the better-established democratic traditions. And "democracy" is what most students reply when I ask about their view of the best form of government—before we get to the *Republic*, that is. When they learn about Plato's contempt for democracy, they are at first surprised, not unlike my students in Montreal. Later they point out, with some discomfort, similarities between the government of Plato's best state and theocratic institutions in Iran, such as the Supreme Leader, the Council of Guardians, and the Assembly of Experts. "But isn't the political ideal of Islam a caliphate with the caliph, the successor of the prophet, as supreme political and religious leader governing the Muslim community according to *sharīʿa* law?" I ask. "Yes," Bisma agrees, "but the Quran also mentions *shūrā*—the ruler's duty to consult with representatives of the people."[18] I suggest leaving aside for now the question of how the consultation mentioned in the Quran compares to modern democratic institutions. "Let's say there is a basis for democracy in Islam, does that mean that democracy is the best form of government?" I explain Plato's comparison between a democracy and a ship of fools.[19] "When it comes to steering a ship, would you trust the captain or the majority vote of the sailors?" Everyone agrees: the captain should be in charge. "So when it comes to steering the affairs of the state, should we trust the majority of the people rather than a wise ruler?" "But we'd lose our freedom if all power is in the hands of such a ruler," Ahmed objects. "So is it better to be free than to be ruled wisely?" I ask.

The *Republic* brings a host of other questions, too. If, for Socrates, to be a just person depends on knowledge of justice, Plato now raises a more fundamental concern: do we have good reasons to choose justice over injustice? This is a radical question in an Islamic context (or a Jewish or Christian one). You can discuss what exactly it takes to be a just person, but not whether walking on "the straight path" (as the Quran puts it in the first sūra) is good for you. All of my students take care not to stray from the straight path. (During a break Bisma shows photos in class, some of which I and the other men are not allowed to see because she appears in them without the veil.) Yet they see how difficult it is to defend the choice of justice for its own sake. (Bisma admits that she would choose injustice over justice once we have clarified Plato's thought experiment, according to which the just person is poor, sick, and ugly, and the unjust not only rich, healthy, and beautiful, but also exempt from punishment.)[20]

First then we must clarify what justice actually means for Plato. The students recognize the affinity between Socrates's ideal of a life based on knowledge and Plato's description of the just person as one ruled by reason. According to the interpretation we agree on, justice consists in two things: the ability to rationally determine what is best for you and the ability to implement it. For the former you need wisdom. For the latter, however, wisdom is not enough; you need *sophrosyne*, that is, self-control in addition to wisdom. For Plato the human soul is a fairly complicated thing. It consists not only of reason but also of irrational emotions and desires. Without *sophrosyne* these will often oppose the instructions of reason and, in the end, gain control. One example Nusseibeh offers is the inability to conquer your anger in the face of an aggressor, even though you know that not retaliating would serve your interests better. In this sense, *sophrosyne* could make an important contribution to solving the Israeli-Palestinian conflict, not only to breaking the vicious cycle of violence that holds the two sides captive, but also to implementing the idea of nonviolent resistance. Nusseibeh explains how he thinks the concept should be applied in the region: faced with nonviolent Palestinian demonstrations, the majority of Israelis would soon recognize that there's no justification to continue the occupation. And would nonviolence not secure the entire world's sympathy for the Palestinian cause? Not everyone in class is convinced. "Isn't it legitimate to respond to violence with violence? Why should the Israelis get away with it?" Amin wants to know. I suggest drawing a distinction: "If someone kills your child, for example, I can *understand* your desire for revenge, because I'd feel the same way; but that doesn't make revenge *legitimate.* And wouldn't prudence recommend nonviolent means if they're better suited for reaching your goal?"

Socrates was enthusiastic about converting all citizens of Athens into philosophers who would ground their lives on knowledge. Plato was much less optimistic (after all, Socrates was put to death for trying). Obviously, children—but also many adults—are, in Plato's view, unable to consistently guide their lives by knowledge. He thus puts considerable effort into developing a pedagogical-political program as a replacement for philosophy among those who are either not yet philosophers or not philosophers by nature. This program includes, for example, religious stories and laws. Whereas the philosopher knows what justice is, the stories make the concept concrete by telling about exemplary just gods or human beings. In this way they convey a less accurate but still useful notion of justice to nonphilosophers. And while the philosopher's actions are guided by knowledge of the good, the laws prescribe good actions to nonphilosophers.

No doubt, there are many reasons to be suspicious of Plato's intellectual elitism—the division of humankind into philosophers and nonphilosophers. That division is, however, central for understanding the interpretation of Islam and Judaism as philosophical religions. Medieval philosophers were able to apply Plato's model to their religious tradition by interpreting the stories and laws of the Torah or the Quran as a pedagogical-political program that philosopher-prophets had worked out to guide the nonphilosophers in their religious communities. When the philosophically gifted members of the community advance in their studies, they can replace the religious stories from their childhood with accurate knowledge that, in turn, can be reconciled with these stories through allegorical interpretation. It was al-Fārābī who first articulated this idea in the context of Islam. Taken allegorically, true religion and true philosophy coincide. Taken literally, however, religion "imitates" philosophy through stories and laws.[21] Consider God's representation as a king in the Bible and the Quran. For the medieval philosophers it's a pedagogically useful imitation of the philosophical doctrine of God: as God ranks first in existence, the king ranks first in the state. While nonphilosophers cannot fully understand the ontological order, they do understand the political order. In this way they grasp something important about God.[22]

Halfway through the term, during our first class on al-Fārābī, the students ask me how they are doing in comparison to my Montreal students. To be sure, many of the questions they ask and associations they have are different from those I'm accustomed to in Canada. But in many ways they are like all students I've known: some excel, some manage, some struggle. Most of the time, the class discussions are lively and focused. They seem also largely free of stereotypes. Sometimes, out of curiosity, the students ask me personal questions; but neither my Jewish background nor my ties to Europe, Israel, and North America have a negative impact on our interactions, at least not that I can tell. I think one reason for this is that although stereotypes and prejudices are probably not dissolved, they are at least suspended during personal conversation. In fact, one of the two top students in the class is a member of the Hamas faction on campus. Of course the suspension of stereotypes and prejudices is not enough. Dissolving them requires something like Socratic examination. But by calling the stereotypes into question the personal encounter may well be the beginning of such a process.

Al-Fārābī saw himself (and was perceived by later philosophers, both Muslim and Jewish) as the one who renewed the intellectual project of Greek philosophy in the context of Islam. This comes out most eloquently in that he was called "the second teacher" (the first being Aristotle). In order to give a home to philosophy in the Islamic world, one important task, of course, was to clarify its relationship to religion. For al-Fārābī there is no conflict between the two; for he takes the prophet, the founder of the religion, to be not only the leader of the community but also a philosopher—in other words, something quite close to Plato's philosopher-king. The prophet provides philosophical instruction to the philosophers in his community and pedagogical-political guidance to its nonphilosophers. Simplifying a bit, one could say that these are the two sides of al-Fārābī's religion: knowledge and education.[23]

So far so good. But there's a problem that the students become aware of after a while. The most important requirement that al-Fārābī's prophet must fulfill is intellectual perfection. How is this compatible with the claim that Muhammad is *ummi*—a term normally rendered as "illiterate," and taken as a proof of the divine origin of the Quran. How could an illiterate person have composed such a sublime book if not through a miracle of God, becoming, as it were, the channel for what the angel Gabriel dictated? The *ummi* issue ushers in a lively discussion. If al-Fārābī is right that divine revelation means attaining complete knowledge, then, indeed, only a miracle can make an illiterate person into a prophet. "But why didn't God just equip Muhammad with intellectual excellence instead of breaking the normal course of nature?" Usman asks. The students then realize that on al-Fārābī's view any philosopher (with the necessary poetic gifts) could have written the Quran. Next we consider the question of whether al-Fārābī's concept of God would allow for miracles at all. God's absolute unity excludes any change in God; that is, God cannot want to interrupt the course of nature now if God didn't want to do so before. "But if he eternally willed a miracle to occur at this time," Ahmed suggests, "then the miracle doesn't imply a change in his will." The discussion continues along these lines for a while.

On the way back to Jerusalem, Nusseibeh shares that he ran into real problems when he taught al-Fārābī in the 1980s as a professor of philosophy at Birzeit University. Because the students did not distinguish between al-Fārābī's position, which he was defending for the sake of argument, and his own position, he was perceived as promoting a heretical concept of prophecy. A few days later an article appeared in the student journal accusing him of introducing "a new prophet at Birzeit." Since then, he tells me, he has never entirely rid himself of the odium of a heretic.

Although al-Fārābī speaks of prophetic religion, he never quite explicitly speaks of Islam. In fact, he has a theory that allows for a form of religious pluralism, though one quite different from those advocated today. For if religion on one level is an imitation of philosophy, there is no reason why a set of true philosophical doctrines cannot be represented by different sets of parables and metaphors. To be sure, the truth is one; but there can be many imitations, some of which may be as good as others. In this sense Jews and Muslims could not only speak to each other as philosophers, but also accept each other's different religious commitments. The students have no major objections to looking at the literal content of Judaism and Christianity as imitations of the truth, because Islam takes both to be based on valid (if superseded) revelations. But what about Buddhism, for example? If Buddha was an accomplished philosopher and poet, there's no reason, on al-Fārābī's grounds, to say that Buddhism is not a religion that, like Islam, contains the truth, but imitates it in a different way.[24]

With Averroes and Maimonides, we finally come to the application of al-Fārābī's model to the interpretation of Islam and Judaism as philosophical religions. At first, the students struggle to grasp that Averroes is actually setting forth an Islamic view. The gap between the Islam they know and this philosophical interpretation turns out to be quite difficult to bridge. Hence they often argue that "according to Islam" this or that is the case, for example that there is an absolute limit to human understanding, or that God can hear although God has no ears. Averroes would reject both claims. But instead of engaging Averroes, they take him to be talking about something other than Islam. When, on the other hand, he speaks of *al-Ḥaqq* (truth) as the criterion for accepting what is written in the books of the philosophers, they automatically identify it with Islam, but without at first seeing the twist that, for Averroes, Islamic views are true because they correspond to philosophically demonstrated propositions. In other words, rejecting a proposition of an ancient philosopher in the name of Islam means to reject it because it is philosophically flawed. As disagreements among philosophers show, they can also make mistakes.

Neither Averroes nor Maimonides openly subscribes to al-Fārābī's religious pluralism. But isn't the fact that they were able to locate the same philosophical world-view in both Islam and Judaism a kind of indirect proof of it? With this the students agree. "But what's your own view of these philosophically reinterpreted religions?" Ahmed wants to know. "Do you buy it?" "There are parts I find attractive," I reply, "but certainly not all of it. I don't believe, for example, that historical religions have a common philosophical core and differ only in how they represent it. For me pluralism requires accommodating real differences." But in other respects, I suggest, we can still learn from Averroes and Maimonides. "If we're genuinely committed to a religious tradition, shouldn't we interpret it in light of the beliefs about the world and the good which, after careful reflection, we accept as true? How else can we do justice to the truth we take this tradition to embody?" "But didn't many Aristotelian doctrines that Averroes and Maimonides endorsed turn out to be completely wrong?" Shirin objects. "Sure," I reply. "So it's very possible that our interpretations will also be overturned in the future. Still, shouldn't we give it our best shot?"[25]

Ahmed has another personal question for me: "Are you an intellectual elitist who looks down on the dumb masses?" "Well, aren't we all nonphilosophers as children?" I reply. "As for adults: doesn't the effort we're willing to put into rational deliberation vary according to inclination, time and other factors?" To illustrate the point, I ask the students to consider two contemporary problems: global warming and the just distribution of wealth. "Wouldn't you agree that we can solve these problems only by observing strict environmental and ethical rules? But how many of us have the necessary expert knowledge—about climate change or about ethics and the economy—to come up with these rules on their own?" "So you think we should enforce them by law?" Usman asks. "No, but couldn't we embed them in religious traditions through interpretation? If you're a Muslim who also cares about sustainability and social justice—wouldn't you want these values to be part of Islam and shared by everyone who's brought up as a Muslim?"

When I leave Israel, the region is once again a war zone—the Second Lebanon War. The excited media display blood, missiles, and body parts; crying families and angry bearded men; soldiers, tanks, and warplanes; ruined buildings and damaged cars; solemn faces making solemn statements. A day before my departure, I call Nusseibeh to discuss the students' final grades. He sounds depressed. But even if the Middle East isn't yet ready to be saved, philosophy can make an important contribution—through rational arguments that can be understood and evaluated without regard to religious or national commitments, through Socratic examination that probes the fundamental notions informing our lives, through teaching *sophro-*

syne, which permits us to translate the insights of reason into practice. Not even those who reject the claim that philosophy is universal can denounce this as "Eurocentric." To be sure, philosophy did not originate in the Middle East; for reasons that I think are contingent, it originated in Greece. But it certainly was integrated into the culture of the region long before the tribes that settled in Europe (Saxons, Franks, Goths, Lombards, and so forth) were seriously exposed to it through Latin translations of Arabic texts.

TEACHING MAIMONIDES IN MAKASSAR

Getting from Montreal to Makassar is no picnic. During our thirty-six hours traveling, between multiple stops, security checks, and baggage retrievals, my wife and I debate whether it is more important to teach public health or philosophy in Indonesia, because this is the purpose of our three-week trip to the capital of the Indonesian province of Sulawesi in May 2007. We both teach at McGill University: my wife is a physician, specializing in public health; I'm a philosopher, working on, among other things, Muslim and Jewish thought. Our classes at Alauddin State Islamic University—one of fourteen academic institutions in Indonesia that make up the public system of Islamic higher education—are part of a McGill-based initiative called the Indonesia Social Equity Project, funded by the Canadian International Development Agency (CIDA). Nobody denies the usefulness of teaching medicine and public health, especially in a developing country. But why does CIDA send a philosopher instead of a second doctor or, for that matter, a social worker, engineer, or economist? Someone, in other words, whose expertise is of immediate use for improving the living conditions of Indonesians? Most people—in Indonesia and elsewhere—don't even know that the problems philosophers turn over in their minds exist. Much less do they feel the need to understand or resolve them. Are their lives any less happy for that reason? Many would say that the opposite is the case.

In fact, philosophy can play an important role in the world's largest Muslim country (of the 240 million inhabitants, about 88 percent are Muslim, equaling the number of Muslims in the entire Middle East). Present-day Indonesia, at least as it presents itself to me, is a gigantic intellectual and political laboratory, where Islam is trying to come to terms not only with democracy (since Suharto, Indonesia's military dictator for over thirty years, was ousted in 1998), but also with the country's long-standing commitment to religious pluralism, modernization, and the construction of a national identity. Coping peacefully with the tensions that this process generates will require a good deal of creative thinking. It is here that the tools of philosophy may prove useful.

About twenty students have signed up for my class. They've parked their motorcycles in front of the building where we got one of the few air-conditioned rooms on the large green campus not far from downtown (everyone rides a motorcycle here—from schoolgirls in uniform to businessmen in suits). All students are doing graduate work in the different departments of the Faculty of Islamic Studies: in Islamic exegesis, history, and education, for example, and a few also in *Uṣūl al-dīn*, the philosophical and theological foundations of religion. Most of them already have families and work, often as teachers in local schools. Because I don't speak Bahasa Indonesian, the country's national language, class discussions take place in Arabic and English. Together we examine the relationship between ethics, politics, and religion: first through Plato and Aristotle, and then through medieval Muslim and Jewish philosophers who creatively adapted the Greeks' conceptual framework to their own purposes. Although the texts are old, the questions they raise are often very much alive for the students. As a consequence, time and again historical and contemporary perspectives blur in the discussion.

Democracy is a hot topic in Indonesia. In a public lecture to faculty and students, I suggest that if I were the Indonesian minister of education, I would make introductory philosophy courses mandatory at all Indonesian high schools and universities. One reason I give is related to Plato's famous thesis in the *Republic*: a good state can come into existence only if the rulers become philosophers or if philosophers rule. For without knowing the common good, Plato argues, one cannot attain it.[1] If Plato is right (and I think he is), it follows that a good *democratic* state must turn all citizens into philosophers.[2] Not everyone in the audience is persuaded. One student remarks that his friend, after studying philosophy, began to behave in a rather peculiar manner: "He would walk around in two different shoes, for example, or put tea into the coffee machine." (Already, upon our arrival, Hamdan

Juhannis—a specialist in Indonesian Islam who comes to receive us at the airport—warned me that jokes about philosophers are widespread in Indonesia.) "Good point," I reply, and mention the passage in Plato's *Theaetetus* where Socrates recounts the story of a Thracian maid who made fun of Thales because he fell into a well while studying the movement of the stars.[3] "But I don't think that's a bad thing—to be distracted by big questions," I add. Others are more amenable to the idea. Wahyuddin Halim, a lecturer in the Department of Islamic Theology and Philosophy, asks me what textbook I would recommend for an introductory class. I suggest turning to Palestinian philosopher Sari Nusseibeh, the president of Al-Quds University in East Jerusalem, where I had taught a class the year before. Nusseibeh developed a course called "Critical Thinking" that is mandatory for all students at Al-Quds.[4]

Another student asks whether the kind of democracy I'm proposing is not a "Western concept" that must remain alien to Indonesia. I protest strongly. To begin with, Western democracies are not grounded on philosophical deliberation.[5] If Indonesia were to achieve this, it would, in my opinion, become significantly superior to any democracy in the West. Moreover, philosophical debate is in many ways an integral part of the Islamic intellectual tradition. From the point of view of contemporary Indonesia, Muʿtazilite *Kalām*, a school of thought that flourished from the eighth to the eleventh century under the rule of the Abbasid caliphs, is an interesting example (though by no means the only one). Harun Nasution (d. 1998), who was one of Indonesia's most influential theologians and public intellectuals, conceived his project of bringing together Islam, rationalism, and modernity in Indonesia as a revival of Muʿtazilite *Kalām*.[6] *Kalām* literally means "speech" in Arabic and refers to the tradition of debating the fundamental principles of religion, for example the existence and nature of God, the origin of the universe, and the question of whether the human will is free or determined.[7] What is distinctive about the Muʿtazilite school of *Kalām* is its commitment to reason. "The first duty prescribed to you by God," writes Abd al-Jabbār, a tenth-century Muʿtazilite thinker, is "speculative reasoning" (*al-naẓar*).[8] Without speculative reasoning, Abd al-Jabbār argues, firm knowledge of God can't be attained. That knowledge, in turn, is the foundation of all other knowledge, since all things are caused by God. Simplifying a bit, one can say that the Muʿtazilites did not accept religious doctrines on the authority of revelation alone, but were confident that they could be confirmed through rational examination. In addition, they also developed a sophisticated culture of debate, not only among themselves, but also with thinkers from competing Muslim intellectual currents and other religious traditions—Jews, Christians, and Manichaeans.[9] Given the pluralistic character of Indonesian society today, this seems to make Muʿtazilite *Kalām* an attractive historical model for conducting contemporary discussions.

"But in which sense can the Muʿtazilites and Harun Nasution really be described as champions of democracy?" objects Wahyuddin Halim. True, certain views of the Muʿtazilites were imposed as state doctrine by the Abbasid caliphs, and Nasution, whose academic career unfolded under Suharto's "New Order," was mainly interested in promoting modernization. On the other hand, some Muʿtazilites were so strongly egalitarian that they came close to anarchism. They insisted that all humans are able to determine good and evil on the basis of the divine law and independent reasoning, and that they have the duty to reject anything contradicting their judgment—even if it is commanded by the Imām, the political leader. The Imām's office, moreover, should be elective and filled by the person of the greatest merit. If the Imām acts against the divine law, he must be deposed. And since, in practice, the corruption of the Imām seemed to be the rule rather than the exception, some Muʿtazilites thought it would be better to get rid of political leaders altogether.[10] Then again, even if democracy wasn't the original purpose, why shouldn't the well-honed intellectual tools developed by Muʿtazilite *Kalām* be put into the service of public democratic debate?

Leaving aside the issue of philosophy, several students question why Indonesians should support democracy at all. Echoing the earlier student, they are concerned that the concept is a Western import. Wasn't democracy brought over by members of the Indonesian elite who had studied in Europe? Or in the schools of the Dutch colonizers who exploited Indonesia for almost 450 years—until its independence in 1949? Is the economic situation not worse now than it was during the New Order of military dictator Suharto? Are not nondemocratic Islamic countries like Saudi Arabia prospering in contrast to Indonesia? I reply that it is by no means obvious that economic prosperity is the same as human flourishing. "Wouldn't many people trade off some wealth for individual rights and political participation?" I ask. And if democracy could function only in the country that originally invented the concept, no country could be democratic except for some parts of Greece. Since the age of ancient Athens, many countries around the world have successfully naturalized democracy, including countries like Germany, Japan, and India, which can hardly lay claim to long-standing democratic traditions.[11] "In any case," I suggest at the end of the discussion, returning to my argument for widespread philosophy education, "whether democracy is a good thing is ultimately a philosophical question. You can't avoid philosophy if you want to come to a conclusion on this issue that's supported by good reasons."

On the other hand, the democratic victories of Islamist parties—for example, the Islamic Salvation Front in Algeria and Hamas in Palestine—show that experiments with democracy in the Muslim world can lead to outcomes in which the West finds little reason to rejoice. "In the upcoming elections for governor in Sulawesi," Hamdan Juhannis tells me, "one of the three candidates is the son of a former leader of the Muslim rebellion in Sulawesi." The son hasn't given up on the father's objectives, but he's using democratic means instead of arms to attain them. "His goal is to turn Sulawesi into a province governed by *sharīʿa* law similar to Aceh where *sharīʿa* law was formally implemented in 2003." In this sense, the future of Indonesian democracy is open, but there seems little reason for immediate concern. The candidate in question was not elected and, in general, since democracy was restored in 1998, parties advocating the establishment of an Islamic state have never attained more than 20 percent of the vote. "But the debate about the value of democracy and its relation to Islam won't end any time soon," Hamdan stresses.

Democracy, however, isn't the only import from the West. Academics spend much time debating the question of "Orientalism," made prominent by Edward Said: did the scholarly study of the Muslim world lead to an objective representation or to an ideological distortion in the service of Western imperialist projects?[12] Whatever the answer, one part of Western culture is well on the way to conquering Indonesia's postcolonial urban soul: KFC (though served here with the ubiquitous rice instead of fries) and similar blessings—Pizza Hut, McDonald's, you name it—enjoy immense popularity here. Just as popular are big shopping malls, sporting the same assortment of boutiques, restaurants, and cinemas as those back home. And this is where quite a few young Indonesians would like to take us. Thus, after three hours of lecturing on philosophy, democracy, and religion, I find myself savoring Pizza Hut's newest culinary creations, strolling through the hippest mall in town, and watching the latest Hollywood blockbuster. "So are you a purist who doesn't want cultures to mix?" Wahyuddin Halim asks me. "Not at all," I reply. "But I don't see anyone reading Shakespeare or Kant or listening to Mozart; that's also part of Western culture." "But who's going to decide what people should appropriate? Should we force them to listen to Mozart instead of Madonna?" Wahyuddin objects. "No, but we can give them tools to make reflected choices. Public health physicians, for example, will tell you that a traditional Asian diet is better than fast food. So from a health point of view going to KFC isn't a good choice."[13]

In class, when we discuss Aristotle's *Nicomachean Ethics*—selections of which we read in a medieval Arabic translation—questions related to consumerism also arise: how much do things we can buy contribute to a good life? Aristotle takes the best life to be one devoted to contemplation.[14] But whether or not we agree with his claim, more interesting is that he conceives practical philosophy as the art of making the right decisions about how to live. This means three things for Aristotle: figuring out what is best for us, figuring out the means to attain it, and developing the moral dispositions (for example, self-control and courage) that permit us to carry it out.[15] "But," objects Ahmad, "if practical reason can do all this, what role is left for religion, in particular for *sharīʿa*, God's revealed law?" That question, I reply, can be put just as well to the Muʿtazilites, who argued for objective moral standards that human reason can grasp. Aristotle, we find out at the end of the *Nicomachean Ethics*, does think that laws can play a crucial pedagogical role in shaping the character of citizens: by prescribing what is right and wrong before practical reason is able to discern it.[16] "But that's not how Muslims view the role of the *sharīʿa*," Ahmad objects. "It depends on who you ask," I reply. "Averroes, for example, claims that the *sharīʿa* embodies practical reason in Aristotle's sense."[17]

Islam—like Judaism and Christianity (although the case is somewhat different for each)—has no standard answer to the challenges of democracy and pluralism. This doesn't mean that Islam is incompatible with them. But making the Indonesian configuration work will require quite a bit of intellectual effort. I for one doubt that the ultimate outcome of the process will be secular as the concept has been understood in the West over the past few decades. Secularization—in the sense of both the separation of religion and state and the large-scale rejection of traditional religion—is certainly not consistent or complete in the West, and this is not the place to discuss its causes (some of which are peculiar to Christianity and to European history). Nor is it right to say that the Muslim world isn't secular at all. With respect to separating religion and state, for example, the situation varies considerably from Turkey to Indonesia to Iran. But on the whole I find it difficult to imagine that Islam will be fundamentally challenged anytime soon, either as a political factor or as the religious commitment of the great majority of Muslims.

Taking a religious framework of one kind or another as given, the challenges and tensions that Indonesia and, more generally, the Islamic world face today raise many important philosophical issues: from political participation, human rights, and pluralism to autonomy and authority in moral action and the relationship between reason and revelation. Muslim intellectuals have discussed variations of these questions since the middle of the nineteenth century. But no matter how sophisticated these discussions are, they largely pass unnoticed in the West (Indonesian intellectuals like Harun Nasution, for example, are virtually unknown here; most of their work is available only in Indonesian).

The West's focus on terrorism and religious fundamentalism (incidentally, only about 10 percent of Indonesians support fundamentalist Islam, and fewer than 1 percent support groups that use terror to achieve their goals)[18] as well as on the stalled Israeli-Palestinian conflict leaves little room for philosophical debate. Are democracy, human rights, and pluralism compatible with Islam? Are there Muslim thinkers who propose good arguments against democracy, human rights, and pluralism? For me, at any rate, the discussions with Indonesian colleagues and students are a good opportunity to consider these questions and revisit the solutions on which we've settled in the West—their historical background and the extent to which they depend on a secular framework.

One of the greatest current challenges to Indonesia's liberal Muslims, such as the professors and students I meet in Makassar, is to reconcile Islam and religious pluralism. The answer they propose aptly illustrates the potential of the discussions taking place in Indonesia today, even though it also raises new questions.

My first encounter with non-Muslim religions in Indonesia is rather disconcerting. It takes place immediately upon our arrival at the bookstore in Makassar's airport (and visits to other bookstores later confirm what we see there). On offer are not only Indonesian translations of Danielle Steele's latest novels and American self-help books about how to get a successful business off the ground, but also a wide range of old and new anti-Jewish texts, including *Mein Kampf*, a history of the Waffen-SS, an abridged version of Henry Ford's *The International Jew* (which comes with a free brochure of *The Protocols of the Elders of Zion*), a book titled *Holocaust—Fact or Fiction?*, and—on the same bookshelf—John Mearsheimer and Stephen Walt's *The Israel Lobby*. Some of the books sport cover quotations and pictures from Iran's president, Mahmoud Ahmadinejad, himself the hero of various monographs. Other monographs are devoted to Hassan Nasrallah, celebrated as the victor of the most recent Israel-Lebanon War. This shows that the almost Gnostic view that identifies a Jewish world conspiracy as the source of universal evil, along with other elements of contemporary Islamist rhetoric, have found their way from the Middle East to Indonesia. But this is a phenomenon of recent years. The attitude informed by such literature is arguably inconsistent with what Robert Hefner calls "civil Islam," which the majority of Indonesian Muslims embrace, and whose most distinctive trait, according to Hefner, is "its remarkable cultural pluralism."[19] Indonesia thus provides an interesting argument for the view that although the rise of fundamentalism has many causes, religion, paradoxically, must not be one of them.

The political, economic, and social problems that, especially over the past decade, have played into the hands of fundamentalists are too complex for a detailed analysis here. They include ethnoreligious conflicts, widespread corruption, economic stagnation, and growing poverty. Radical preachers, such as Indonesia's notorious cleric Abu Bakar Bashir, exploit the situation to further their cause: because Indonesia is not ruled by Islamic law, they claim, it does not enjoy God's favor, which, in turn, is the reason why so many Indonesians struggle. And members of the country's corrupt elite, in their view, are nothing but puppets, ultimately controlled by Jewish masters.[20] In reality, things look much more prosaic and involve neither God nor the Jews. Many of the current problems are the legacy of the Suharto regime, combined with the 1997 East Asian financial crisis, of which Indonesia was one of the principal victims. Suharto managed to channel more state money into the pockets of his family and friends than any other corrupt political leader. He pushed economic privatization and other measures on the advice of the so-called Berkeley mafia (Indonesian economists trained at Berkeley), which led to the temporary growth of the economy, but mostly benefited foreign investors and a few local helpers. Needless to say, the regime, thanks to its business-friendly economic policies and violent anticommunism, enjoyed wide support among Western countries.[21] We get to see some of Indonesia's wealthy in Jakarta at a luxurious shopping mall, complete with a Starbucks café, located next to our hotel. Here the elite come to buy Chanel's new perfume, Sony's PlayStation 3, or the latest Western fashion. The wealthy can also be found on the route from the hotel to the university, in a neighborhood of lavish villas commonly known as Jakarta's "Beverly Hills." "Most of the time, only the servants live here, while the owners are abroad," comments our taxi driver.

Whatever the causes of fundamentalism, I want to know why it does not fit with the way Islam is understood by most Indonesian Muslims. Whereas in Egypt (where I studied Arabic for three months in 2000) I found a mix of anti-Zionism and anti-Judaism to be pervasive—from the street to the university to the media to the museums—I encounter nothing of the kind among the faculty and students I meet in Indonesia. On the contrary: when, for example, I mention in class that Jewish thinkers in the Middle Ages made important contributions to all major Muslim intellectual currents, several students express surprise that they were never exposed to Jewish sources. Burhanuddin suggests that I recommend to the rector including such sources in the curriculum for the future.

The question of Islam's relation to Judaism in Indonesia is part of the broader question of Islam's relation to other religions. In itself it's not a pressing issue, given that an Indonesian Jewish community does not exist and that the Arab-Israeli conflict is far away. There is evidence that a basic commitment to the kind of religious pluralism promoted by the state is shared by about 60 percent of Indonesian Muslims.[22] During our three-week stay in Indonesia we witness two national holidays: one is the day of Christ's ascension, the other *Waisak*, the birthday of Gautama Buddha. On this occasion, official boards throughout Jakarta display congratulatory messages to the Buddhist community.

What, then, sets Indonesian Islam apart from the Islam of other regions in the Muslim world? For one thing, Islam arrived here quite late and not as the consequence of military conquest. Introduced by Muslim traders from India and elsewhere, it began to spread in a mostly peaceful manner from the thirteenth century onward. The space of its diffusion was anything but homogeneous: an archipelago of some seventeen thousand islands populated by more than three hundred ethnic and linguistic groups that never came together to form a centrally administered Islamic state (indeed, for most of the Islamic period Indonesia was under Dutch colonial rule). In addition, Islam blended with a wide range of previously existing religious traditions. Most important among these is the Indigenous Animism, as well as Hinduism and Buddhism, which had been Indonesia's state religion in earlier periods. As a result, forms of Islam developed that differed significantly not only from each other, but also from mainstream Islam in the Middle East. To quote from Clifford Geertz's description of *abangan*, the religious syncretism prevailing in Javanese villages, "Hindu goddesses rub elbows with Islamic prophets and both of these with local *danjangs*" (guardian spirits, such as Nini Tawek, the angel of the Javanese kitchen).[23] *Abangan* is one of three main forms of Javanese religiosity that Geertz distinguishes in his highly controversial *The Religion of Java* (1960). Although I haven't met anyone in Indonesia who accepts his analysis without reservations (he is taken to be saying that most Indonesians are not authentic Muslims), the peculiar character of Indonesian Islam is now widely recognized and plays an important role in the academic discussion of religious pluralism.

McGill University, it is worth noting, has had considerable impact on the development of this discussion. The McGill-Indonesia connection dates back to the 1950s, when Muhammad Rashidi became a visiting professor at McGill's Institute of Islamic Studies, one of the most renowned centers for the study of Islam in the West. Rashidi, who obtained a doctorate in Islamic studies from the Sorbonne in Paris, had been Indonesia's first minister of religious affairs when the country declared independence in 1945. Since Rashidi, dozens of Indonesians have graduated with MAs or PhDs from McGill, a substantial number of McGill professors have taught in Indonesia, and bilateral research projects exist on a wide range of academic subjects. Many McGill graduates have gone on to play important roles in Indonesia's intellectual and political circles. They include Harun Nasution, whose neo-Muʿtazilite project first took shape at McGill, and Mukti Ali, the minister of religious affairs from 1971 to 1978. Mukti Ali's term overlapped with Harun Nasution's tenure as the rector of Jakarta's State Islamic University, and together they managed to implement a radical and controversial reform of the curriculum for the public system of Islamic higher education. Whereas before it was modeled on the curriculum of al-Azhar University in Cairo, the foremost center of Islamic scholarship in the Middle East, they rewrote it along the lines of the curriculum at McGill. Over time the twin pillars of McGill's Institute of Islamic Studies were adopted by the Indonesians: the interdisciplinary study of Islam and the comparative study of religion. The impact of all these efforts is discernible on three levels: the "official" Islam promoted by the ministry of religious affairs, the discourse about Islam shaped by intellectuals like Harun Nasution, and finally the perception of Islam on the grassroots level, since the Islamic universities recruit their students mostly from pious and economically disadvantaged sectors of Indonesian society. Many of the students, moreover, later become teachers in high schools (as I mentioned above, most of the graduate students in my class are already teaching), thus further disseminating what they have learned.

The main group competing with the scholars in the State Islamic Universities are Indonesia's *ʿulamāʾ*—scholars of Islam usually trained in traditional Middle Eastern centers of learning, such as al-Azhar University. The *ʿulamāʾ* always looked with suspicion at their colleagues, who mostly graduated from McGill and other universities in the West. "They accuse us of being Orientalists!" I am told by Fuad Jabali, the director of graduate studies at the State Islamic University in Jakarta (whose doctorate is from McGill). "But the paradox is that only Western universities provide the intellectual freedom to study the rich and dynamic Islamic tradition in all its manifestations. There we can acquire the methods for understanding how these manifestations vary according to historical, cultural, socioeconomic, and geographic circumstances." Recognizing and contextualizing the diversity of Islam instead of artificially constructing a monolithic orthodox tradition—the approach of the *ʿulamāʾ*—has nowhere proved more liberating than in Indonesia. Harun Nasution's two-volume work, *Islam Considered from Different Perspectives*, published in 1974 while he was rector of the State Islamic University in Jakarta, articulated the new scholarly agenda in a programmatic way. For one thing, it allowed students to understand Indonesia's Muslim practice as one of many legitimate expressions of Islam, rather than as a deviation from the alleged orthodoxy of the Middle East. At the same time, it provided a foundation for the concept of pluralism, both within Islam and for Islam in relation to other religions—most importantly, other religions practiced in Indonesia: Hinduism, Buddhism, and Christianity. This is the background to the concepts of relativism and inclusiveness—key concepts that inform the argument for pluralism set forth by Nurcholish Madjid (d. 2005), one of the most influential contemporary Muslim thinkers in Indonesia. ("What people write now," says Wahyuddin Halim, "are just footnotes to Madjid.")

It's no accident that the most interesting discussion I have with the students about religious pluralism occurs when we look at the notion of a plurality of valid religions proposed by al-Fārābī.[24] For the way various contemporary Muslim intellectuals like Nurcholish Madjid combine the universal and the relative in their conception of religion has interesting affinities (and even indirect historical links) with the Platonic tradition represented by al-Fārābī. According to al-Fārābī, Plato argues for the existence of multiple divine laws. Al-Fārābī explains this by drawing on a comparison that Plato and Aristotle make between the statesman and the physician. The physician always seeks the same outcome for his patients, namely to restore their health. Health, of course, is a universal good. But the regime prescribed by the doctor will vary according to the specific conditions of the patient. A good statesman, who for al-Fārābī must be both a philosopher and a prophet, proceeds in a similar way. But whereas the physician aims only at the health of the body, the statesman aims at the citizens' well-being as a whole, which, according to al-Fārābī, depends most on moral virtues and scientific knowledge. Although he takes moral standards and scientific doctrines to be universal, the ways of conveying them to citizens through laws and education differ. Each way is valid within a particular set of conditions—historical, cultural, social, geographic, and so forth. The particular instantiations of this universal content, in turn, are the multiple existing religious traditions. From this point of view, teaching the medieval Jewish philosopher Maimonides in Makassar becomes interesting indeed: the students recognize that Maimonides's interpretation of the Law of Moses can be seen as applying al-Fārābī's theory to Judaism, making Judaism one such instantiation that can exist alongside Islam as another.

But even more interesting are the similarities that the students identify between the view set forth by al-Fārābī and the understanding of religious pluralism proposed by Indonesian intellectuals, in particular Nurcholish Madjid. On the one hand, the wide range of historical manifestations of Islam is taken to reflect different interpretations of the Quran and the *Sunna*, which are equally valid within their specific contexts. This allows, for example, acceptance of the divergences between Indonesian and Middle Eastern Islam as contextual rather than essential. On the other hand, Islam as a whole is taken as only one historical expression of God's eternal and universal religion, on par with other historical religions. "The Divine Message itself, not in its essence, but in its response to the demands of times and places, is historical and, therefore, subject to change," writes Madjid.[25] As Basnang explains in class, "The Quran, the *Sunna* and their interpretations are one way to implement this eternal and universal religion. Hinduism, Buddhism, Judaism and Christianity are other ways. What they all have in common is that they originate in God and lead the members of the community to God, guided by divine revelation."

In a sense, this student's view just takes one step further the traditional Islamic recognition of Judaism and Christianity as valid but, since the advent of Islam, superseded revelations. This recognition had already been extended to the Manichaeans in the early Islamic period. The Indonesian model, however, abandons the concept of supersession and extends the recognition to additional religious traditions. Basnang's explanation reflects quite accurately Indonesia's official stance on religious pluralism, institutionalized in the principles that make up *Pancasila*, the five foundational doctrines of the Indonesian Constitution. From a religious point of view, the first principle is the most important: it prescribes the belief in the one and only God. Thus according to *Pancasila*, being a Muslim is not a requirement for being an Indonesian citizen, but being a monotheist is. It took the Hindu and Buddhist communities in Indonesia several years to persuade the authorities that their religions are monotheistic and that they received a divine revelation. At the same time many Indonesian Muslims interpret *Pancasila*'s first principle as a minimalist definition of Islam.[26] In this broad sense, then, all Indonesians can be seen as Muslims and as living under Islam's rule. This is an interesting attempt to reconcile the commitment to an unconditionally valid core of Islam with religious pluralism. The result is rather different from the religious pluralism advocated in the West.[27] Indonesia is not Canada. Yet the result bears witness to the hermeneutical flexibility of Islam and the industriousness of Indonesians in working out solutions that, here at least, secure the generally peaceful coexistence of a wide range of religious communities. In this sense, Maimonides's interpretation of Judaism against the background of al-Fārābī's conception of a plurality of valid religions seems to agree more with Indonesia's commitment to religious pluralism than the anti-Jewish discourse recently imported from the Middle East (where, in turn, it had earlier been imported from Europe). At any rate, as we're waiting for our return flight from Makassar to Montreal at the end of our stay, the assortment of anti-Jewish literature in the airport's bookstore looks a bit less unsettling to me.

On the other hand, the boundaries of the solution show that making pluralism work in a nonsecular Muslim country like Indonesia may well require an additional intellectual effort. Adapting Hinduism and Buddhism to a monotheistic framework certainly demands a good deal of force. Atheists are excluded from the outset. Adherents of religions not recognized by the state, in particular Animism, "have no religion," explains Sabir. But besides the problem of inclusiveness, there is also the problem of conceptual coherence. The students simply take for granted the truth of the important historical religions up to Islam. ("If there are conflicts between religions," says Burhanuddin, "they come from false interpretations; the problem lies in the commentaries, not in the sources.")

But they don't have a criterion to distinguish between a true religion and one that is false. I press them repeatedly to explain why they reject the Bahá'í religion, founded in the nineteenth century by Bahá'u'lláh, as "merely human." Why is Muhammad's claim to have received divine revelation true, whereas that of Bahá'u'lláh is false? And why is Muhammad taken to be the "seal of the prophets"? On the assumption shared by the students that God adapts his message to varying historical circumstances, why should he have stopped doing so after getting to seventh-century Arabia? Has the world not changed since then? That's precisely how Bahá'u'lláh justifies his prophetic mission. Why, moreover, is following a false religion prohibited? (Fatira mentions an Indonesian woman who was recently jailed for claiming that she received divine revelation.) Are we forbidden from making mistakes? These are tough questions at a State Islamic University in Indonesia, and they leave the students fairly perplexed. Perplexity, of course, can also be a gate into philosophy. And some more philosophical reflection might be needed if the students want to turn their present commitments into a defensible position.

At least some of them are up to the challenge. On my last day in Makassar, Hamdan Juhannis tells me that a student, who happens to be his neighbor, did not sleep for two nights because he couldn't stop thinking about the issues we raised in class.

SPINOZA IN SHTREIMELS

AN UNDERGROUND SEMINAR

"I'm sitting in my armchair," Abraham, a Hasidic Jew from New York, tells me on the phone. He is a Satmar (the most insular of all Hasidic sects) and is calling me in Montreal where I sit—less comfortably I suspect—in my McGill philosophy department office. I don't laugh right away, so he adds, "Don't you do philosophy in an armchair? I'm ready to give it a try!" And then a cascade of big questions (and answers) pours over me: Does God exist? (He doubts there's a proof.) Are space and time finite? (He thinks they are infinite and wonders if the creation story is a myth.) Do we have good reasons to observe God's commandments? ("If there's no God, perhaps as social conventions?") I do my best to keep pace, apparently to his satisfaction. A friend of a friend who heard that I was interested in doing philosophy with people who are not academic philosophers had given Abraham my number. "I have a group of friends who may be interested," he says. "We're kind of an underground debating club."

A couple of months later I move to Princeton to take up a fellowship at the Institute for Advanced Study for the 2009–10 academic year. Once settled, I call Abraham to organize our first meeting. We meet at the Star Bar, a trendy lounge in SoHo. Abraham and two friends—Isaac, a fellow Satmar, and Jacob, a Lubavitcher—wink at me from their bar stools. Their black attire stands out in the hip crowd that has already gathered for an after-work drink. Jake, the bartender—Chinese letters tattooed on his fingers, an unlit cigarette in the corner of his mouth—pours us a draft beer that we take with us to the management office on the second floor, where Moshe and Miriam, a Lubavitcher couple, are already waiting for us. Moshe owns the property. He made money in the diamond trade and then invested in real estate. Abraham, who deals with professional electronic equipment, proudly points out that the bass drums we hear through the floor come from a sound system bought from him.[1]

"So what's in it for you?" Moshe asks me as we sit down. "I'm trying to find out if one can use philosophy to address real-life concerns and to have debates across cultural boundaries," I explain, somewhat professorially. "The clash between modernity and religious tradition, for example, gives rise to fundamental questions. And I want to know if philosophy can help to explore them."

We are all a bit nervous. I hand out the syllabus. We will start with Plato's *Apology* and *Euthyphro* to meet Socrates and discuss the idea of an examined life and the nature of moral norms. Then we will read the *Deliverance from Error*, the intellectual autobiography of al-Ghazālī, the great eleventh-century Muslim thinker. "How do you pronounce his name?" Jacob asks. "Just add an 'i' to *chazal*" (the standard Hebrew acronym for the scholars of the Rabbinic period, *chakhameinu zikhronam li-v'rakhah*, our sages of blessed memory), I reply, and they laugh.

In the *Deliverance*, al-Ghazālī describes how he lost his childhood faith and eventually doubted even his ability to grasp things through his senses and intellect, until God restored his trust in his cognitive faculties. It is a great text to start a discussion of the foundations of knowledge and of the relationship between reason and faith. We will pursue these issues from a Jewish angle through Maimonides and Spinoza, whom they have already read. Finally we will discuss Nietzsche, nihilism, and what might come after the loss of faith.

My Hasidic students nod seriously in agreement. They have been struggling to find answers for years, while maintaining their busy professional and family lives. (At one of our meetings, the Satmars can barely keep their eyes open after a nightlong philosophical discussion with a friend from abroad.) So this is not merely an academic exercise for them. "From the point of view of our community," Isaac explains, "studying these books is much worse than having an extramarital affair or going to a prostitute. That's weakness of the flesh, but here our souls are on the line—*apikorsus* (heresy) which means losing our spot in the *olam ha-ba*ʿ (hereafter)." That spot may well be lost anyway for my Hasidic students. They are modern-day Marranos of reason: God-fearing Jews in public, freethinkers in secret.[2] At one of our last meetings I ask them to think about how Plato, Maimonides, and Spinoza would respond to Ivan's claim in Dostoyevsky's *Brothers Karamazov* that if God is dead everything is permitted. "Thanks," Isaac replies. "Now at least I've something to keep my mind busy at shul on Shabbos."[3]

When Abraham asks me how I became interested in their world, I tell them that while I am not attracted to its content, I am intrigued by its form—a world that revolves around wisdom and God, rather than wealth, sex, power, and entertainment. Since they take philosophy to be a secular project, they are surprised when I say that from Plato to Spinoza most philosophers endorsed this ranking, though not the same accounts of wisdom and God. And they are stunned to learn that I would be very disappointed if my six-month-old daughter grew up to value lipstick, handbags, and boys in sports cars more than education and ethics. "In some ways you seem to be *more* Satmar than we are!" Isaac exclaims. "Though I don't want her to wear a wig, have seven children, and owe obedience to her husband," I quickly add. Still, my idea of a good life calls into question what they have learned about the secular world. Throwing off the yoke of the Torah, it turns out, needn't translate into hedonism.

Of course my Hasidic students are not the only ones with misperceptions. When the hip crowd at the Star Bar meets them, all they seem to see is sexual repression. One evening, after discussing Plato for three hours, we go down for a drink. A young filmmaker from the neighborhood—disheveled red curls, carefully groomed tousled look—approaches us to ask if my students would be interested in appearing in her next art film: "I'm dying for a scene with Hasidic men being seduced by a sexy blonde!"

At the end of our first meeting I pass around copies of the *Apology* and the *Euthyphro.* Jacob asks me to send them an electronic version of the texts as well—"makes it easier to read on the Blackberry." "Our Rebbe went through all this effort to protect us from the pollution of the outside world," Isaac says, "and then came the Internet!" As much as the rabbis would like to ban it, their hands are tied: "We can't do business without the Internet and we can't support the community without business." Of course the rabbis prohibit going online for private purposes. "But how can they enforce that?" Isaac asks. "When the last ban came out, it was posted on 'Hasid and Heretic' and got some thirty hilarious comments!"

"Hasid and Heretic," a website maintained by a "conflicted soul, torn between the world of Hasidism and the world of reason," is one of several anonymous online forums for disaffected community members like my students. Other sites they tell me about include "Hasidic Rebel" and "Unpious: Voices from the Hasidic Fringe," remarkable for its cutting-edge design. "We know that we're not alone," Abraham says, "but we have no idea how many of us are out there, since we all live in camouflage."

We discuss Plato under the inquisitive eyes of Rabbi Menachem Mendel Schneersohn, the last Lubavitcher

Rebbe, looking down on us from several pictures in Moshe and Miriam's living room, where they have reserved "the philosopher's armchair" for me. "Not all pictures are kosher though," Miriam says. One in which the Rebbe is wearing a light-colored gray hat caused a stir every time family visited. "So we put it away." Their apartment in Crown Heights, the center of the modern Lubavitch movement, is our workshop's second venue. Like the Satmars, the Lubavitchers are a Hasidic sect with roots in Eastern Europe. But while the Satmars are the champions of seclusion, the Lubavitchers practice *kiruv*—religious outreach to bring all Jews back to the Torah. This, they believe, will usher in the coming of the Messiah. We had to postpone our meeting at Moshe and Miriam's because their downstairs neighbor had added a visit at the Rebbe's gravesite to the celebration of his son's *bar mitzvah* (many Hasidim do so to ask the Rebbe to intercede with God on their behalf). "People would have started talking if we hadn't showed up," Moshe explains.

As I mentioned earlier, for my Hasidic students philosophy is a secular project. So they find Plato's *Apology* confusing. Aren't reason and religion at odds? Why, then, is Socrates so pious? Not only does he present his philosophical enterprise as a divine mission, but he chooses *Kiddush Hashem* (martyrdom) over disobeying God's command! "He can't have been bluffing for other Athenians," Isaac observes, "since they executed him for impiety. If his piety was just for show, I'm sure he would have done a better job!" Then another idea occurs to him: "Maybe Socrates died too early?"

Now it's my turn to be surprised. "Well," Isaac explains, "I didn't lose my faith all at once, but layer after layer. It started with doubts about the things people believed in our community. So I went back to the *rishonim* (medieval commentators on the Bible and the Talmud). But they also said things that didn't add up. So I went back to the Talmud. In the end, all I was left with was the Bible. For a while I was proud to rely only on the true divine source while everyone else was deceived by misleading human interpretations. I felt real joy at a *hakhnasas sefer Torah* (the festive procession escorting a new Torah scroll from the scribe's house to the synagogue). When I finally lost trust in the Bible as well, it was as if the ground had broken away under my feet. Maybe if Socrates had lived longer, he would have gotten to this stage."

Abraham suggests a different interpretation: "Since all Socrates got out of his philosophical investigations was that he knows nothing, he finally took a leap of faith." "But if Socrates was really just a pious skeptic, why is he so fond of a philosophically examined life?" I ask. "Perhaps asking questions gave him perverse pleasure," Isaac replies. "When I started asking questions, our rabbis told me that it was the urge of a corrupt soul."

"Or could one interpret Socrates as a *moderate* skeptic?" I ask. "When he claims to know nothing, perhaps he means nothing with absolute certainty. Then debating beliefs would be useful, because it allows us to get rid of false ones and to be more confident about those that weren't knocked down, even though they might be refuted later."

"But what if someone convinces us that a true belief is false and a false belief is true?" Miriam asks. "Good point," I say, "that's why Plato doesn't trust rhetoric. In addition to debating techniques, you also need debating virtues. You have to love the truth more than winning an argument."

"So couldn't we say that from a Socratic standpoint it is an advantage to be born into the Hasidic community?" Jacob suddenly asks. "If you're a Hasid in New York you can't help but reflect on what you think and do since almost everybody else thinks that you're weird. But if you're more or less secular and more or less liberal, chances are that you'll never get challenged since almost everybody else agrees with you." He has a point. On the other hand, any debate about values within the Hasidic community is suppressed. "When you started asking questions," I point out, "you had to go underground. But Socrates wants you to ask these questions, and he likes to debate them in public."

I propose that for Socrates we all want to live well and how we actually live depends on our beliefs about the good life. "So getting these right is crucial. And we can't just rely on the authority of tradition. We have to think things through on our own, guided by reason. And since God for him is reason, a life guided by reason is at the same time a life guided by God."[4]

My students can, of course, see the problem with relying on the authority of a religious tradition. All of them have rejected the idea of the good life with which they were brought up. In their communities, a good life is a life devoted to serving God. This is accomplished through study, meticulous observance of God's commandments, and devotion to the Rebbe, who helps the community get in touch with the divine. The desires of the body, by contrast, are strictly regulated, lest they distract from worship. "But if you think that this is all wrong, why don't you just leave the community?" I can't help but ask.

One reason is practical: when the last layer of faith finally falls away it is usually too late. As Isaac puts it, "By then you speak mainly Yiddish, you're married, have children and you're a *talmid chakham* (rabbinic scholar) with no marketable skills." Jacob—who like me is in his late thirties—misses one meeting because of his twentieth wedding anniversary (I haven't yet reached my second). When he got married, he was a brilliant yeshiva student, poised to become a Talmud scholar—"the dream son-in-law," he says ironically. "You know what I wanted from my father-in-law as a wedding gift? That he pay for ten more years of Talmud study!" They all know of people who could no longer bear the cognitive dissonance and left the community. "But none of them managed to build a happier life outside," Jacob says.

And if there were no practical hurdles, would they leave? From the armchair, I suggest a thought experiment: "Suppose you could go back in time and exchange your life for that of anyone in the hip crowd that comes to the Star Bar—would you do it?" They hesitate. The truth is that they have come to enjoy the thrill of leading a double life. They are also successful in their jobs. And they take pride in the existential and intellectual depth they were able to achieve by struggling with their lives' contradictions. "This bohemian culture looks colorful on the surface," Jacob says, "but we're grappling with the big questions: God, reason, Torah, the meaning of life!"

The trouble is that you cannot bring up your children as Marranos of reason. I tell them how becoming a father helped me to get clearer on the beliefs and values I wanted to teach my children. They, on the other hand, must applaud when their children succeed by standards they have secretly rejected. "It can be heartbreaking," Isaac says. "So people in our situation often avoid having more children." Although the use of contraception is prohibited in their communities (the purpose of sex is to be fruitful and multiply, as commanded in Genesis 1:28), the issue is not publicly raised, and childless couples or couples with fewer children are generally presumed to have medical problems. "The worst," Isaac says, "is if the spouse is not on board." He tells me about a friend who stopped having sex altogether because his wife did not agree to using contraception. Jacob points out how harsh an indictment of their world this is: "In effect I guess we're saying that it is better not to live at all than to live a Hasidic life."

Isaac is the youngest and unhappiest of the group. He is planning to enter the business world like Abraham,

Moshe and Jacob, but before that he still has to get through a second year of Talmud study—a gift from his father. Cutting short his studies would be frowned upon, so he reluctantly goes on. "I'm not sure if discovering that I'm living in a prison was a blessing or a curse," he says. "Most people I see around me seem much happier than I am." He has decided to let his children grow up in the system to spare them his inner turmoil. "Under some circumstances, lies seem to provide a better life than truth."

Moshe and Miriam try to accomplish a balancing act with their two children. Their daughter now attends a Lubavitch school for girls in Crown Heights. "But then she wants to study medicine at Columbia," Miriam says proudly. Their son, in turn, is fascinated by the theory of evolution. "We don't let religion set limits to their intellectual curiosity," Moshe explains. When Moshe reminds his son that according to Jewish tradition God created all animal species in two days, he replies, "I know, but I'm talking scientifically, not biblically." "And which one is right?" Moshe asks. "The Bible of course!" he answers without hesitation. "That's the default assumption," Moshe says with a hint of concern.

They know that they are treading a fine line. On my way back to Montreal, at the end of the year, I visit them in their summerhouse in the Catskills, and they tell me that their daughter is attending a special Lubavitch camp. Recently she has also gotten involved in *kiruv* activities. "When I was her age, I was just as zealous," Moshe notes. "I hope it's just a phase."

Back at our secret meetings in New York, Abraham expected Socrates to be easier going. He is surprised to find him chastising Athenians for caring more about the well-being of the body than the well-being of the soul. "You'll have no better luck with Plato," I tell the group. "He compares our appetites to a 'multicolored beast' that the faculty of reason has to control."[5] "What about Epicurus?" Abraham asks. "Doesn't he say that the best life is a life of pleasure?" "That's true," I concede, "but he argues that the greatest pleasure doesn't lie in satisfying our appetites, but in the peace of mind we reach when we are satisfied and free from irrational fears—the fear of death, for example, and the fear of divine retribution. So we're best off if we find satisfaction in a simple life lived in the company of philosopher-friends."[6]

Plato's psychology reminds Moshe of a distinction between the "animal soul" (*nefesh behemit*) and the "intellectual soul" (*nefesh sikhlit*) made by the founder of Lubavitch Hasidism, Rabbi Schneur Zalman of Liadi, in his chief work of Hasidic philosophy, the *Tanya.* The distinction surely doesn't come from the Bible. But could it have come from Plato? Jacob notes that there is also some concern among the Lubavitchers about the similarity between the *Tanya*'s description of moral character and Aristotle's. One explanation people in the community give is that Aristotle studied Torah with the rabbis. "That's like al-Ghazālī!" I say. "He turns Aristotle into a disciple of ancient Sufis to justify borrowing from his ethics."[7] The historical truth in Rabbi Schneur Zalman's case is that he read classical medieval Jewish thinkers like Saadia Gaon, Judah Halevi, and Maimonides, who were steeped in the Arabic theological, scientific, and philosophical literature of their time. That literature, in turn, often built on Greek sources. "The Hasidic authors of course weren't aware of these contexts," I explain. "So Rabbi Schneur Zalman wouldn't have known that he was picking up an idea from Aristotle."

"How could the medieval thinkers get away with interpreting the Torah according to Aristotle or the Sufis?" Jacob wonders. "Well," I say, "they thought that if Judaism is true, it must agree with every true insight, even if it came from a Greek or a Muslim. Today's Haredim, on the other hand, think that they have to shelter true Judaism from any supposedly corrupting outside influence." This leads us to discuss whether the Haredi fight against cultural contamination is a lost cause from the start. I point to an interesting passage in *Toledot Yaakov Yosef*, the first published Hasidic book, by Rabbi Yaakov Yosef of Polnoye, a disciple of the founder of Hasidism, the Baal Shem Tov. Rabbi Yaakov Yosef draws a contrast between a "small" and a "great" struggle; the former refers to a battle with weapons, the latter to the moral wrestling of the soul with the "evil inclination" (*yetzer ha-ra'*)—our base desires. The source of the metaphor is actually a famous hadith frequently cited by Sufi mystics: the Prophet Muhammad tells a group of soldiers that after returning from the "smaller *jihād*"—the *jihād* of the sword—they now must take up the "greater *jihād*"—the *jihād* of the soul against pleasure. Naturally, the Baal Shem Tov and his disciples didn't study the Sufi masters. But they did study Bahya ibn Paquda's *Duties of the Heart*, which was translated from Arabic to Hebrew in the twelfth century and became a classic of Jewish thought. Bahya's account of the soul's ascent to God was strongly influenced by Sufism and includes a version of the hadith in question, without, of course, the reference to the Prophet Muhammad.[8] As Isaac points out, excitedly, the Satmar Rebbe, Joel Teitelbaum, was also a devoted student of Bahya's *Duties of the Heart*!

Where do they come down on the *Euthyphro* question? Do moral norms depend on God's will, or does God want them because they are objectively valid? To clarify the question, Isaac says, "Consider our friend Moshe here. Is Miriam attracted to him because he's objectively beautiful or is he only beautiful to her because she loves him?" In the *Euthyphro*, Socrates seems to be committed to the objectivist view. The gods love that which is holy or good because it is, in fact, just that. "That would mean that there's no need for revelation," Jacob says. "We don't need God to tell us that tomatoes are red, so we also wouldn't need him to tell us that stealing is bad."

"But what is it in the act of stealing that is objective like the color of a tomato?" Abraham asks. "I can't see that stealing is bad the same way I can see that tomatoes are red. So if revelation is out, and if we can't show that moral judgments are objective, then they must be subjective." Most modern philosophers, Abraham suggests, are relativists. "Of course we don't always act on our desires, but that has nothing to do with objective facts; it's just the social context. You don't steal because you're afraid the police will catch you. Would we continue observing the *mitzvos* (divine commandments) if we were on a desert island and didn't fear the community's response?"

On this point I disagree with him. "If you ask the hip crowd at the Star Bar, a lot of them might turn out to be subjectivists or relativists about morality. I'd guess many will say that what's good for one person needn't be good for another. But neither of the two major schools in contemporary moral philosophy—Kantians and consequentialists—defend relativism. Kantians, for example, argue that moral norms are absolutely valid: whether you're under the eyes of a police officer or on a desert island—stealing is always wrong."[9] "So the bottom line," Jacob cuts in, "is that even if we throw off the yoke of the Torah, few philosophers would say that we are free to do as we like."

Al-Ghazālī begins *The Deliverance from Error* with an account of how he lost faith in the authority of "parents and teachers"—that is, the beliefs and values stemming from the contingent circumstances of our socialization.[10] This happened when he realized that he might have been just as fervent a Jew or Christian as he was a Muslim, had he been brought up in a Jewish or Christian community. Jacob describes a similar childhood experience: "I would get up very early to study Torah for a couple of hours before *shacharis* (the morning prayer). On the way to shul, I noticed that Muslims were already praying at the mosque. So I asked myself: if we're both passionate enough about our religion to get up while it's still dark—how can I be sure that my religion is true and theirs is false?"

If al-Ghazālī can't rely on the authority of his religious tradition, what can he rely on to attain knowledge? We discuss Plato's classical definition of knowledge as "true, justified belief." Why doesn't a true belief qualify as knowledge, regardless of its justification? Moshe reports a conversation he overheard in the synagogue between two elderly Lubavitchers. "They were discussing a text by Rabbi Schneur Zalman that said that most of the earth is covered by water. 'That's a strange thing to say,' one of them commented, 'but if the *Alter Rebbe* said so, it must be true.' So they had a true belief, but clearly not knowledge!"

Al-Ghazālī's problem was that he came to distrust both the senses and the intellect. The senses tell us, for example, that the sun is the size of a *dinar* coin. Here the intellect can identify and correct the mistake. But can we really trust the intellect? We can conceive of a higher cognitive faculty, al-Ghazālī argues, that would identify the mistakes of the intellect in the same way as the intellect identifies the mistakes of the senses. The fact that we don't have such a faculty or know about such mistakes doesn't mean that we don't make them, since we also wouldn't know about the mistakes of the senses without the intellect. Al-Ghazālī's skeptical crisis ended only when God cast light into his heart, restoring his trust in his cognitive faculties. "Does that mean that you can't get from skepticism to philosophy without the help of God?" Jacob asks. It's a good question. "Perhaps an alternative is to settle for something less than *absolute* certainty," I reply. "But doesn't that put philosophers at a disadvantage, compared to rabbis, priests, and imāms who claim they've access to God's infallible message?" Jacob wants to know.

Although studying Maimonides's chief philosophical-theological work, *The Guide of the Perplexed*, is prohibited in their community, my Hasidic students have all read parts of it in secret. The great twelfth-century philosopher and rabbi is a bit like a Trojan horse of reason inside the gates of rabbinic tradition. His monumental *Mishneh Torah*, the first systematic code of Jewish law, is on the shelves of every yeshiva. But his reinterpretation of Jewish beliefs and practices in light of views derived from Greek and Muslim philosophers collides with today's ultraorthodox idea of the Torah's purity and self-sufficiency.

"Some of our rabbis say that Maimonides wasn't really a philosopher; he only used it because the members of his community were so confused by philosophical ideas," Isaac explains. "Others say that a genuine Jewish philosophy exists, but teaching it to the masses is strictly forbidden. But most agree with the Vilna Gaon that the 'accursed philosophy' led Maimonides astray."

The Gaon's ire was sparked by Maimonides's claim that the only benefit of reciting a charm over someone bitten by a snake or a scorpion is that it puts the mind of the superstitious at ease. How dare Maimonides explain away the countless stories in the Talmud in which miraculous charms reveal God's power?[11] Isaac shows me a photo of an advertisement in Yiddish that he saw at Christmas: "*Zu farqoifen a machalah oder a tsarah for a arel*" (For sale an ailment or a misfortune for a non-Jew). "No wonder that our rabbis side with the Gaon!"

For my Hasidic students, Maimonides's bold reinterpretation of Judaism in light of his philosophical views played an important role at the first stage of their gradual alienation from their community. "He gives you the confidence to reject all kinds of superstition—for example that our Rebbe can miraculously heal or foresee the future," Isaac says. "And many of the biblical stories that people in our community take literally turn out to be prophetic parables according to Maimonides."

My students, however, did not become Maimonideans. Modern Orthodox Jews often revere Maimonides as a model for reconciling Torah (revelation) and *madda*ʿ (reason). My Hasidic students don't buy it. All attempts to integrate secular life and Jewish tradition ultimately ring false to them. In a sense they keep the Torah and the secular world as strictly apart as their rabbis do; they only have switched allegiances (secretly at least). Moshe tells me about a Lubavitcher friend who led a double life for years. "During the day he was a brilliant Talmud teacher, during the night he explored Manhattan's culture and art scene. Then he became Modern Orthodox and started teaching in a more liberal Yeshiva. But he still doesn't believe in any of it."

They have a good laugh when I tell them about the Yom Kippur sermon I heard in Princeton's reform synagogue. The female rabbi argued that there was no contradiction between obeying God and personal autonomy. The *mitzvot* must convince us that observing them is beneficial for us. ("If you want a day off from email, cell phone, and other disturbances—keep Shabbat!") What God tells us to do coincides with what we really want to do. "Let's hear how good a case a piece of bacon can make for *kashrus*," Isaac jokes. When I say that I have no qualms about circumcising my son, Abraham is surprised: "Why would you do such a thing if you don't believe in the *bris shel Avraham* (Abrahamic covenant)?"

They also doubt that Maimonides truly believed he had bridged the gap. "Did he really think that Moses was a great philosopher?" Isaac asks. "Wasn't he just bluffing to escape the anger of the masses?" They are more attracted to Spinoza. Jacob mentions an old Hebrew book on Spinoza's life and thought by Hillel Zeitlin, a Jewish writer and intellectual who was raised as a Lubavitcher and strongly identified with Spinoza after losing his childhood faith. In the last chapter, Zeitlin claims that central ideas in Spinoza can also be found in Maimonides and other Jewish thinkers.[12] "But Spinoza was more honest than Maimonides," Jacob says. "He didn't pretend that his views fit with traditional Judaism. That's why he was excommunicated."

"But is it true that Maimonides was only bluffing to protect himself?" I ask. "Why did he spend so much time on halakha and reinterpreting Jewish beliefs? Maybe he was a kind of philosophical reformer who wanted to put the Jewish community on a firm intellectual foundation." I also express doubts about their contrast of the insincere Maimonides with the bold Spinoza. "Sure, Spinoza was excommunicated, but after his excommunication most of his close friends were progressive Christians. And his portrait of Christ as a great philosopher sounds a lot like Maimonides's portrait of Moses. Maybe he also wants to philosophically reform religion, not get rid of it altogether."[13]

"But what's the purpose of all this?" Jacob asks. "My sense," I reply, "is that while Maimonides and Spinoza didn't want religion to interfere with reason, they also thought that most people just can't live a rational life on their own. So they tried to make religion into something like reason's handmaid: it should offer guidance to those who aren't capable of being perfectly rational without meddling in the affairs of the mistress." They find the idea interesting, though they can't see how such a project can be made to work in the communities they know, communities defined by their rejection of all things secular.

At the same time, Spinoza is fascinating to them not only because he is a fellow lapsed Jew. They also hope to find in him a philosophical expression of Jewish ideals—from the love of God to the quest for peace and justice—that doesn't require the baggage of traditional beliefs and practices. Abraham, Isaac, and Jacob even join me at a Spinoza conference that Dan Garber, the distinguished scholar of early modern philosophy, has organized in Princeton. Their presence causes puzzlement among the professional philosophers. "Should I have ordered kosher food?" Garber, whose grandfather studied in a yeshiva in Vilna, asks. He then tells a famous joke about a Hasid who arrives in heaven and finds a superb restaurant operated by Moses and supervised by God himself. "I'll have the fruit platter," he says, concerned about *kashrut.* Another Jewish colleague asks me in surprise, "Did I just see a Hasid eating non-kosher potato salad at the buffet?"

During the lunch break I find Abraham chatting with the eminent analytic philosopher Harry Frankfurt (well known outside of academia for his best-selling little book *On Bullshit*). Frankfurt tells Abraham about the Talmud classes he is taking at the Jewish Learning Initiative on campus now that he is retired. "So tell me," says Abraham, seizing the opportunity, "aren't Spinoza and the Talmud at odds when it comes to the truth? Spinoza is sure that he has grasped the truth; he only tolerates disagreement because he thinks that most people aren't able to get it—so he grants them the freedom to make mistakes. The Talmud, on the other hand, says about the disagreements of Hillel and Shammai, '*elu ve-elu divrei Elokim hayyim*' (these and these are words of the living God)."[14]

Frankfurt isn't convinced that Spinoza and the Talmud are at odds. "Even if two philosophers differ, they would be speaking the words of the living God for Spinoza as long as they genuinely seek the truth," he claims. When Abraham asks for my opinion, I say that I think Frankfurt is wrong. "I can't see Spinoza allowing disagreements in the divine intellect."

What does Nietzsche mean when he claims that "God is dead"?[15] I suggest he means the breakdown of what we used to see as the natural and moral order anchored in God—the framework for our judgments about what is true, good, and beautiful. "So I think we experienced nihilism," Isaac says. "The foundation of our faith crumbled and we realized that what we believed in was just a myth organizing life in our community." He tells about a friend who, when he decided that he was living a lie, threw the writings of the Satmar Rebbe on the floor—a symbolic gesture of contempt. "When a Torah scroll is dropped by accident," Isaac explains, "we must fast for forty days!"

But how far are they willing to go with Nietzsche? Socrates, al-Ghazālī, and Maimonides all tried to replace discarded, childish beliefs with new and better ones that were still grounded in God. Nietzsche, on the other hand, makes a stronger claim: there is no objective order at all, only blind, aimless, ever-changing forces of nature. My Hasidic students aren't sure. "I'm an optimist," says Abraham, "I still think that one day I'll come up with definitive answers." I suggest that Nietzsche might dismiss this as fear to embrace life in a world devoid of objective meaning. "But Nietzsche could be wrong," he replies. "How can he be sure? Spinoza says that there's an objective order without assuming that things follow a divine plan established by a transcendent God."

Nietzsche's main concern, however, was that worldviews grounded in God give rise to a morality that cripples our life here and now for the sake of an illusory afterlife. Rather than realizing our potential on earth, we are taught to be humble, obedient, and self-sacrificing to secure a place in heaven.[16] "That's true for us," Isaac says, "but is it also true of biblical religion? The Bible doesn't really distinguish between body and soul and certainly doesn't take the good life to be the soul's reward in heaven; living well means flourishing on earth—being blessed with wealth, a beautiful family, and so forth." I suggest taking his argument one step further: "Maimonides not only rejects traditional views of the afterlife, but also divine reward and punishment in this world; he claims that Moses uses these threats and promises the way a teacher uses them—to direct people to the true love of God. Once you get there, you no longer need fear of punishment and hope for reward as motivation; loving God is its own reward. Or take Spinoza who says that the intellectual love of God—which is to say nature—is the highest good, no matter whether the mind is immortal."[17]

"So why does Nietzsche reject any objective standard of human excellence, not just the ones involving heaven?"

Jacob asks. "For Nietzsche a good life is one in which you realize your own nature with its particular set of instincts and desires," I reply.[18] "In our community it's the exact opposite," Isaac says. "The more you desire something the worse it is; it's the *yetzer ha-ra*ʿ trying to distract you from serving God." But is the difference really so glaring? "Nietzsche," I suggest, "is just as much a champion of self-control as Plato or Maimonides. Can an *Übermensch*, a 'superman,' be enslaved to his passions? Take the Jazz band, for example, that is playing tonight at the Star Bar: doesn't it take a lot of disciplined effort to become a good musician? When Nietzsche equates a noble life with a powerful life he doesn't mean power over others, he means the ability to reach one's goals without being diverted by lust and fear."[19]

Moshe points to a similar concept in the work of Rabbi Schneur Zalman: "He distinguishes between *teva*ʿ (nature) and *hergel* (habit). The idea is to reshape your nature through habituation: getting rid of features that prevent you from attaining your goal and acquiring features that help." I suggest that the only thing Nietzsche would disagree with is the goal, which for the *Alter Rebbe* is, of course, *avodat ha-Shem* (serving God).

"Being an *Übermensch* sounds stressful," Isaac says. "Nietzsche," I counter, "might be critical of you if you allow family and community ties to hold you back from realizing yourselves. To be free for him also means to be free from social attachments."[20] "But isn't there a problem?" Isaac asks sharply. "Nietzsche's excellence is always about outdoing others; doesn't that create dependence on those outdone?"

Miriam finds Nietzsche's praise of solitude implausible. She sides with the tradition from Plato to Spinoza that claims that one cannot live, let alone live well, without living with others.[21] "And why is he so anxious about the weak? The weak for Nietzsche always seem to be out to trap the strong. But can't helping the weak also be a sign of strength?" We return to Maimonides: as a brilliant philosopher, legal scholar, doctor, and community leader he sounds like a Nietzschean *Übermensch*. He may even have had as much contempt for the masses as Nietzsche did, but he spent most of his life trying to raise the Jewish community to a higher intellectual and moral level. "For Maimonides, sharing perfection with others was another way of imitating God," I explain.[22]

At our last meeting we discuss Nietzsche's idea of eternal recurrence. Below us the Star Bar's DJ of the night is skillfully juggling two beats. "If Nietzsche is right, we'll be having this exact same discussion again and again and again," I say. "So we don't have to feel sad about our meetings coming to an end?" Jacob jokes. Like me they are not really convinced by the thesis, but fascinated by the thought experiment Nietzsche lays out in *The Gay Science*: Imagine a divine messenger who reveals to you that "this life, as you now live it and as you lived it in the past, you will have to live again and another infinite times; and there will be nothing new, but every pain and every pleasure, every thought and every sigh, and every unspeakable smallness and greatness of your life will come back, in the same sequence and order." What would you do—"gnaw your teeth and curse him," or say "you are a god, I've never heard anything more divine!"?[23]

CITIZEN PHILOSOPHERS IN BRAZIL

Getting out of the cave and seeing things as they really are: that's what philosophy is about, according to Almira Ribeiro, the person most passionate about philosophy I've ever met. Ribeiro teaches the subject in a high school in Itapuã, a neighborhood on the outskirts of Salvador, the capital of the state of Bahia in Brazil's northeast. Although Itapuã is celebrated for its beauty by some of Brazil's greatest singers—Dorival Caymmi, Vincius de Moraes, Caetano Veloso—parts today are also poor and violent. Ribeiro had planned to introduce her students to the Pre-Socratic speculations about nature among the white dunes and lush vegetation around Lake Abaeté, but the open-air class was cancelled because of security concerns.

Most of the four million slaves shipped from Africa to Brazil were sold in Salvador, the first residence of Portugal's colonial rulers. It's still Brazil's blackest city. In Ribeiro's neighborhood, children play football or do *capoeira*, pray in Pentecostal churches, or worship African gods. Many are involved with drugs. "Every year we lose students to crack," she tells me.[1] And they study philosophy two hours each week because of a 2008 law that mandates teaching philosophy in all Brazilian high schools. Nine million teenagers now take philosophy classes for three years.

"But seeing things as they really are isn't enough," Ribeiro insists. As in Plato's parable in the *Republic*, the students must return to the cave and apply what they've learned. There's no shortage of opportunities for this in Itapuã. The contrast between the new luxury hotels along the beach and the neighborhood's overcrowded streets gives rise to questions about equality and justice. Children kicking around a can become a starting point for a discussion about democracy: football is one of the few truly democratic practices here; success depends on merit, not class privilege. Moving between philosophy and the world they inhabit, the students can revise their views in light of what Plato, Hobbes, or Locke had to say about equality, justice, and democracy, and discuss their own roles as political agents.

To foster that discussion, Ribeiro must battle a deeply rooted political defeatism. "All politicians are thieves," I hear time and again. Voting in Brazil is obligatory, but many think it's useless. In 2010, the largest number of votes for any member of congress went to Tiririca, a popular TV clown suspected to be illiterate. He ran on the slogan "I don't know what a congressman does, but vote me in and I'll tell you." João Belmiro, another high school philosophy teacher, finds this outrageous. Philosophy, he hopes, will bring change before long.

"There are also other ways of political participation," Ribeiro tells her students. She gives them the town hall's phone number for complaints about infrastructure and asks them to find something in their street they want repaired. When one student calls, nothing happens. But when fifteen call, the city reacts. "You see that pothole?" she asks me. "It's been closed. And that street lantern? It's been fixed. Thanks to our philosophy class! Politicians can't afford disgruntled citizens who will vote them out of office." That's how Ribeiro enlivens concepts like democracy, power, and rights. She's used the strategy herself in the past. To get the street she lives on paved with asphalt she sent a long list with residents' signatures straight to the mayor. In the same vein she's now organizing an association of philosophy teachers. One urgent matter is the lack of qualified personnel. Another project is improving the relationship with the philosophy department at the Federal University of Bahia (UFBA), the region's academic hub. Most teachers I meet complain that academic philosophers ignore them or look down on them. "From the ivory tower things down here look pretty messy," says João Belmiro.

That's not surprising, considering that the 2008 law is above all a political project. In 1971 the military dictatorship that ruled Brazil from 1964 to 1985 eliminated philosophy from high schools. Teachers, professors in departments of education, and political activists championed its return, while most academic philosophers were either indifferent or suspicious. The dictatorship seems to have understood philosophy's potential to create engaged citizens; it replaced philosophy with a course on moral and civic education and one on Brazil's social and political organization ("to inculcate good manners and patriotic values and to justify the political order of the generals," as one UFBA philosophy professor I know recalls from his high school days).

The official rationale for the 2008 law is that philosophy "is necessary for the exercise of citizenship."[2] The law, which is the world's largest-scale attempt to bring philosophy into the public sphere, thus represents an experiment in democracy. Its advocates argue that philosophy produces the critical skills without which democratic debate and decision making are a sham. Among teachers, at least, many share Ribeiro's hope that philosophy will provide a path to greater civic participation and equality. Can it do even more? Can it teach students to question the foundations of society?

I was intrigued when I first heard about the law and wanted to see for myself whether philosophy could be efficacious outside of academia. The opportunity came with a sabbatical in 2010. My path to this subject is both intellectual and personal. I am an academic philosopher in Canada, with Brazilian roots: my parents were activists in a Marxist student group opposing the dictatorship and fled before I was born, though we returned to Brazil for four years after the 1979 amnesty for political refugees. With the help of professors and students from the UFBA philosophy department, I gain access to a broad range of schools in Salvador, where I am welcomed as a guest teacher and have the opportunity to discuss with other teachers their curricula, instructional styles, and hopes for the students.

In every classroom I am at first flooded with questions: Who is this professor from Montreal and what's he doing here, the students wonder. I quickly learn that my excitement about Brazil's experiment with philosophy is not universally shared. "Learning how to read and write and basic mathematics is useful," Márcio, a tenth grader, says. "But why should I care about Plato's concept of the soul?"

I concede to the class that learning philosophy for the sake of erudition may not be the best use of their time. "But if you want to build a just and democratic society, isn't it useful to get as clear as possible on what you mean by justice and democracy and to examine if you have good reasons to pursue these?" I ask. "And aren't your intuitions about knowledge, goodness, and beauty worth investigating?"

Well, perhaps. But first the students have more questions for me. Is it true that Canadian bacon is the best in the world? What do people abroad think about Brazil? How did I get into philosophy? And—still more personally—do I believe in God, a question I encounter in nearly every classroom. I try to get out of it by mentioning Spinoza's God. That doesn't mean much to the students and, truth be told, I don't even believe in the impersonal God of Spinoza. "We knew it—all philosophers are atheists!" they reply gleefully. When I ask who is a Catholic, who is an Evangelical, and who practices the Afro-Brazilian religion Candomblé (Salvador alone has more than two thousand *terreiros*, Candomblé houses of worship), all students raise their hand at least once.

Because of Marx's pervasive influence on the humanities and social sciences in Brazil, academics often dismiss religious beliefs as opium of the people. Some philosophy teachers avoid talking about religion altogether. Others get caught between the fronts. One teacher tells me that she advised a student, confused about Darwin, to endorse evolution in exams while secretly holding on to man's descent from Adam and Eve. "That's how I do it," she explains. João Belmiro has no patience for such games. "I don't care if people say that religion is everyone's private affair; it's great material for philosophical discussion." He feels that something important is at stake. "Some kids say that philosophy comes from the devil; I try to show them that it is only opposed to *false* religion." As we pass by a group of Evangelical students who are holding hands in a circle and praying, he grumbles that this should be prohibited in schools. "People pay the *dízimo* (a tenth of their income) to the church ministers who promise to solve their problems by casting out a demon or something like that. That's superstition, not religion!"

During the ninety-minute bus ride to a high school on the outskirts of Salvador, after the expensive high rises, shopping centers, and chichi restaurants along the city's beach strip lie behind me, I spot a Pentecostal church on every block. "But the Evangelical movement has good side effects," Almira Ribeiro says. "The students learn how to interpret a text through studying the Bible. And they don't get involved in drugs."

I assure the students that until the nineteenth century hardly any philosopher was an atheist. Plato's *Euthyphro*—with its argument about the relationship between ethics and the will of the gods—gets us into a lively discussion. "Do moral norms depend on God's will?" I ask them. "Would it be fine to murder an innocent child if God says so?" The students find the idea outrageous. "But doesn't God order Abraham to sacrifice Isaac?" I go on. There is a moment of confusion. "But Abraham also holds God responsible when he wants to destroy Sodom and Gomorra," Luciana replies. I concede that this can be interpreted as an independent norm of justice. "But if God must submit to objective moral norms, do we still need the Bible for moral guidance?" I press on. Pedro doubts that reason can replace the Bible: "Reason even justifies killing innocent people if that's the only way to avoid greater harm."

We assume for the moment that reason is indeed unable to ground absolute moral norms. "But how can we act on the authority of the Bible if there are so many different interpretations of it?" I ask. João intervenes: "Can't each interpretation be right in its own time and place?" I remind them of Salvador's Museum of Modern Art, which they visited on a class excursion. It is located in a beautifully restored *casa grande*—a colonial plantation owner's mansion—with adjacent slave dormitories, the *senzala*.

"You remember the private chapel? Going to mass and having slaves obviously wasn't a contradiction back then." Most students have slaves among their ancestors and thus are reluctant to concede that an interpretation of the Bible allowing slavery is valid. "So is reason the arbiter between competing interpretations?" I ask.

We haven't reached a conclusion when the bell rings, but we have touched on a wide range of important issues in an open-ended Socratic discussion that seems well suited to the public philosophy envisioned in the 2008 law. By giving students the basic semantic and logical tools they need to clarify their intuitions and to analyze arguments for and against their views, philosophy could help to extend and refine the debate that naturally arises in a pluralistic society from conflicting interests, values, and worldviews. And it could also help citizens make wise use of the power they have in a democracy, as Almira Ribeiro's town hall exercise shows.

But can philosophy really become part of ordinary life? Wasn't Socrates executed for trying? Athenians didn't thank him for guiding them to the examined life, but instead accused him of spreading moral corruption and atheism. Plato concurs: Socrates failed because most citizens just aren't philosophers. To make them question the beliefs and customs of their upbringing isn't useful because they can't replace them with examined ones. For Plato, then, Socrates ended up pushing them into nihilism.[3] To build politics on a foundation of philosophy, he concludes, means not turning all citizens into philosophers, but putting true philosophers in charge of the city—like parents in charge of children.[4] I wonder, though, what would happen if citizens were trained in dialectic debate from early on—say, starting in high school. Might they react differently to someone like Socrates? Perhaps the Brazilian experiment will tell.[5]

The Socratic approach does not, however, have much support among the two main camps competing to define the high school curriculum in Brazil: academic philosophers on the one hand, and political activists and educators on the other.

For academic philosophers, philosophy is not a democratic practice or an emancipatory exercise, but a rigorous scholarly discipline. According to the narrative I hear time and again, philosophy in Brazil started in the 1930s, when French scholars founded the philosophy department at the University of São Paulo.[6] They put an end to the "dilettante period" characterized by the oratory of lawyers and the scholasticism of priests that had dominated Brazilian philosophy until then. The most influential French philosophers were Martial Gueroult and Victor Goldschmidt. They argued that doing philosophy was no longer possible, only history of philosophy: reconstructing systems of thought through a painstaking analysis of their immanent structure. Since then, studying the history of Western philosophy has been the paradigm of serious philosophy in Brazil. In one bookstore in Salvador, I find a whole wall filled with successive editions of the series *Os Pensadores* (The thinkers): a remarkable achievement of São Paulo's historical school that made the philosophical classics accessible to everyone in good Portuguese translations. A living philosopher like Sartre, by contrast, was dismissed as frivolous (*L'Être et le Néant* was first translated into Portuguese not by a scholar, but by journalist Paulo Perdigão).

When the first edition of *Os Pensadores* appeared in the 1970s, Brazilian philosophy was undergoing a large-scale transformation that academic philosophers proudly call "professionalization." Research was where the perks lay, as departments began to be evaluated according to quantitative criteria—publications, theses, grants, and so forth. Dozens of academic journals and philosophical societies came into existence. Today there are thirty-eight graduate programs in place, collaborating in a wide range of national research groups. All this is coordinated through the Brazilian Philosophical Association (ANPOF), whose fifteenth biannual meeting takes place while I'm in the country. Some fifteen hundred papers are presented in a week. As I leaf through the six-hundred-page catalogue of abstracts, I realize how sophisticated academic philosophy in Brazil has become. From antiquity to the most recent trends in Europe and the Anglo-Saxon world—everything is covered by state-of-the-art contributions (as I'm on the bus to Almira Ribeiro's high school in Itapuã, a plenary session is being held in the conference hotel on "Tradition and Modernity in Japanese Thought"). Impressive, too, is the assortment of recent scholarship translated from English, French, and German that I find in Salvador's academic bookstores. From these heights philosophy in high school can indeed seem like a millstone around the neck of academics who are dealing with the pressure to "internationalize"—the main challenge of the future according to a programmatic paper circulated at the meeting.

Political activists and educators charge academic philosophers with "intellectual schizophrenia," as Eduardo Oliveira, who teaches in UFBA's Faculty of Education, puts it. "If we want to think we must put on a German, French, or British head; the Brazilian head won't do." Like many in this camp, Oliveira is affiliated with the "philosophy of liberation" movement, a series of loosely related intellectual exercises in resisting local dictatorships and what is seen as domination by the West in political, economic, and cultural spheres. This movement draws on many sources, from Marx to Levinas. It emerged in South America in the 1960s and 1970s together with the pedagogy and the theology of liberation.[7] "It's a dynamic movement with an immense body of literature, some three thousand titles," Oliveira explains. "But our philosophers sniff at it." He tells me about a guest lecture by Karl-Otto Apel, one of Germany's foremost philosophers, best known for his work on discourse ethics, which he developed with Jürgen Habermas. Apel was keen to compare discourse ethics with the ethics of liberation. "The auditorium was packed; the whole philosophy department was there." But when the floor was opened for discussion, Oliveira recalls, there was only embarrassing silence. "So I asked a question and got a friendly reply—followed by more silence. After my third question Apel lost patience, put on his hat and said 'I'm afraid nobody else here's interested in South American philosophy,' turned around and left." Yet whatever the merits of the philosophy of liberation, I wonder if any substantive philosophical agenda is compatible with the diverse views citizens hold in a democracy.

Among the greatest skeptics of the 2008 law is José Arthur Giannotti, one of Brazil's most respected academic philosophers. He is a close friend of former president Fernando Henrique Cardoso, who vetoed the law when it was first proposed in 2001, after it had already been approved by the legislature. "Teaching philosophy to students who can hardly read and write," Giannotti said in an interview on the occasion of the institution of the law, "is sad foolishness."

To be sure, conditions are dire in public schools. Overworked and underpaid teachers deal with students who are often in class for the free lunch and reduced bus fare, or because of former President Luiz Inácio Lula da Silva's welfare program, the *bolsa familia* (family fund). More than twelve million poor families get tiny financial incentives to keep their children in school. Brazil still has fifteen million illiterate citizens and an additional thirty million "functionally" illiterate ones who can decipher a text but not understand it, much less write something coherent.

This doesn't discourage UFBA philosophy students like Vera Malaquias. After putting two sons through college, she left a lucrative job as an accountant and is now studying philosophy and ancient Greek. Her own life experience gave rise to philosophical questions: "The white family of my father met me with suspicion because of my black mother and vice versa—except for my black grandfather who showed me off as his 'white' granddaughter because I inherited few African traits," she tells me. To complicate things her white relatives were wealthy Catholics who looked down on the Pentecostal churches where her black family worshipped. "I was very confused about who I was, what was right, how to worship, and so forth. Over time I was able to translate that confusion into philosophical questions." She tried to organize a workshop on philosophical texts for evening students in a high school—domestic maids, taxi drivers, construction workers, and others who study after the workday, hoping that the high school diploma will get them out of what Almira Ribeiro calls "slave work." "Not one student showed up," Malaquias says. "Then I realized that they were hungry after a long day's work and went straight to the school kitchen." Why not combine philosophy and food, she thought and renamed her workshop "Philosophy in the Kitchen." But also over a meal the students weren't keen on reading and writing. "So I decided to show films as a starting point for philosophical discussion. After all, everyone can watch a film over dinner and express an opinion."

For regular daytime students such creative approaches aren't necessary, and they are outraged when I mention

Giannotti's statement. For them it leads straight into a vicious circle. They argue that one can't establish a just society democratically without citizens knowing what justice is, and that citizens can't know what justice is without philosophy. So if studying philosophy, in turn, presupposes justice (for example, a decent education for everyone), then you can't achieve justice democratically in an unjust society like Brazil's.

The philosophy law presented academic philosophers with a fait accompli, so mostly they've been vocal in ensuring that the high school curriculum reflects their idea of rigor. The *Curricular Guidelines*—published by the Ministry of Education in 2006, as the law was heading for final approval—reflect a broad consensus: high schools should adopt a toned-down version of the academic program with history of philosophy as its "cornerstone."

When I ask Almira Ribeiro what she thinks about these guidelines, she looks amused. "Let's see what my evening class students will say if I ask them to make a structural analysis of Kant's *Critique of Pure Reason*." Even if that were possible, she doesn't see the point. "If the students can't relate what they learn to their own experience—of what use will it be to them?"

Other teachers, however, feel that they must follow the guidelines if they are to be taken seriously. "That's what distinguishes a teacher with a philosophy degree from a charlatan who organizes superficial debates on this or that question of the day," one teacher tells me.

But in a conversation I have with UFBA philosophy students, Laiz points out, "Nobody really thinks that high school students can get through Kant's *Critique of Pure Reason*. That explains the ubiquitous use of didactic manuals." The idea seems to be that if you can't read Kant, the next best choice is to read a Kant digest by a recognized authority. After a précis of the history of Western philosophy, these manuals usually summarize what the author takes to be the principal areas of philosophy. In the most popular manual I see, each chapter is followed by questions for the students. The teacher's version includes an appendix with the correct answers. In the worst case this will lead to rote learning (one teacher goes so far as to give students multiple-choice assessments that include the question of whether Sartre's nationality is German, Swedish, French, or Russian). That approach, in turn, fits the general teaching culture in Brazil. Nelson, another UFBA student, explains, "Since the goal is to get students into university, teachers must cram everything into their heads on which they will be tested in the *vestibular*, the entrance exam."

To be sure, the history of philosophy can help expand our repertoire of concepts and arguments or help us question the things we take for granted: nothing better than Plato's *Republic* to think again about equality, freedom, and democracy. "But the way Gueroult and Goldschmidt interpret texts doesn't allow that," Nelson replies. "They claim that you can't take arguments out of their historical context and treat them as contributions to an ongoing philosophical debate."

This contextualism, too, seems to have left a mark on how philosophy is taught in high schools. In one school, after listening to a glowing student presentation on Aristotle's ethics, I point out that Aristotle, while surely a great philosopher, also argues that women are inferior to men and that some of us are slaves by nature. "Well, that's how people thought back then," the students reply. But I don't let them off the hook so quickly. "Aristotle isn't just repeating the common opinion of his time," I stress. "Plato, his teacher, argues the opposite: that biological gender differences don't mean that women are inferior to men."[8] I also remind them that Aristotle's claim about natural slaves was used to justify slavery in South America.[9] "So what Aristotle said has had a real impact on your own history."

When I try to discuss with members from the UFBA philosophy department some of the concerns about the role of academic philosophers in implementing philosophy in high schools, I get a sense of how sensitive this issue is. One professor even denounces me as an agent of American cultural imperialism and proposes to ban me from campus! Others, however, are sympathetic to the questions I raise. Genildo da Silva, a Rousseau scholar, says that the high school curriculum has been an opportunity for him to think about something new. He feels wary of the academic system's pressure to specialize: "Everything turns around Rousseau—my MA and my

PhD, my graduate students, the conferences I attend, the volumes I edit." Retiring to a farm outside of Salvador and reconnecting with the spirit of his ancestors ("my great-grandmother belonged to an Indian tribe from this region," he explains) is an escapist fantasy that he has been having more frequently in recent years. His parents' dream was to see him, one of seven children of a cacao plantation worker, ordained as a priest. The Catholic seminary he attended sent him to study philosophy for two years at the University of Ilhéus, the capital of Bahia's cacao trade. "We weren't allowed to complete the course, because the Church feared that philosophy would lead us astray," da Silva says. Thanks to a special permission from the bishop, however, he was able to continue—and indeed gave up theology soon after. "In the end," he admits, "philosophy undermined my faith." He points out that many of his colleagues also came to philosophy through the Church. The scholastic curriculum of the Jesuits is Brazil's oldest philosophical tradition, and priests were prominent in philosophy departments until a few decades ago. "My church was associated with the theology of liberation that fuses Marx and the gospel," he tells me. Although he dropped the gospel, he held on to social activism, working in the church's organization of landless rural workers and in education. "When I was accepted to do graduate work at the University of Campinas, one of Brazil's foremost centers of academic philosophy, I felt at first as if a dream was coming true," he says. He proposed a project on the philosophy of liberation. "But I quickly learned that for academics this isn't serious philosophy. So I switched to Rousseau."[10]

To be sure, Brazil offers plenty of real-life experiences that could be addressed in a philosophy class. Consider the myth of racial equality, the idea that Brazil is a "racial democracy." Following the Socratic call to self-knowledge, João Belmiro asks his students to sketch their biography and family background. "They always know much more about the white members of their family than about the black ones," he observes. One white colleague told me that his black wife doesn't like to go with him to the beach. "People think she's a prostitute going out with a gringo." Another white colleague can't bring his black wife to his parents' house. "They're poor and uneducated; she has a master's in history and directs an archive of rare manuscripts from the colonial period." In a country where races are thoroughly mixed, what does it mean that skin color remains important?

Brazil's beach culture, in turn, raises questions about the good life. After teaching in a high school, I walk back to the university campus in the company of three (male) UFBA philosophy students. We are immersed in a philosophical discussion as the street reaches the beach. Suddenly philosophy gives way to poetry: my three companions begin to sing the praises of Brazilian beauty. "If you could choose between a beautiful body and a beautiful law—say, a law that ends social injustice in Brazil—which one would you choose?" I ask them. "The law," they reply after reflecting a bit. "Though I'd be gnashing my teeth," one of them adds, laughing. "So you agree with Plato in the *Symposium* that moral beauty is superior to beautiful bodies?" I ask.[11]

Or consider the gap between rich and poor in Brazil, one of the world's widest. Many here don't perceive it as unjust. In an elite private school in Salvador, philosophy teacher Luis Rusmando tells me, "You've come to the most expensive and bourgeois school in town." An Argentinean Marxist who once wanted to be a guerrilla combatant (two relatives, he told me, were killed by Argentina's military dictatorship) and joined the fight for agricultural land redistribution when he first got to Brazil, he doesn't quite know how he ended up at this school. Although about 80 percent of Salvador's population are Afro-descendants, the only black people I see in Rusmando's school are cleaners and kitchen personnel. "Most of my students think that inequality is a law of nature," he explains. That's why they find nothing wrong with the social hierarchy that Plato proposes in the *Republic*. "Only when I tell them that wisdom, not money, rules, according to Plato, they're confused." Rusmando is also in charge of the students' voluntary community service program. Every few months he drives out to a farm owned by one student's family. "It's amazing how naturally a sixteen-year-old takes charge of the twenty servants who work there," he tells me. The students bring donations to a local daycare and spend a few hours with the poor kids. "For most of them it's an opportunity to party." But he also notices the students who haven't yet lost the ability to be surprised, and to question their narrow world of privilege. "Perhaps that's why I paradoxically feel close to my students," he says.

Back in the public schools, I find that João Belmiro's students take a very different view on inequality and justice. In 1888 Brazil was the last country in the Americas to abolish slavery. "But what is freedom worth," Fernando asks, "without access to land, jobs and education?" All students in his class are in favor of affirmative action programs in universities. The deterioration of the public school system in recent decades, which also left-leaning governments have done little to reverse, has made it all but impossible for poor children to get into one of the coveted public university programs—mainly engineering, law, and medicine—that open the door to wealth and prestige.

"But are quotas enough?" I ask the students. "Isn't there a risk of graduating black engineers, lawyers, and doctors who think and behave exactly like their white colleagues?" If philosophy is indeed the way to change such attitudes, as the students propose, what should it aim at? It turns out to be quite difficult to say how much equality social justice requires.

"Consider two *acarajé* stands," I say, referring to Salvador's most popular street food. One is run by a talented cook, the other by a cook without talent. Both work hard, but the first stand has lots of customers, the second only a few. "Would it be just to take part of the talented cook's income and give it to the untalented one?" Differences due to talent or effort seem acceptable to the students as long as equal opportunities are granted. I press harder: "Isn't talent an arbitrary fact of nature? Why, then, should it be rewarded? And is effort really more in our control? If one cook has just lost a child in an accident and now is depressed and can't work properly—does she deserve to be punished?" The bell rings. One more inconclusive discussion, and another invitation to continue the philosophical conversation.

WORD-WARRIORS

PHILOSOPHY IN MOHAWK LAND

"So who's the savage here?" Gilbert Terrance asks. He is a Mohawk from Akwesasne, one of the largest Mohawk reserves in North America. A visit to St. Joseph's Oratory, Montreal's famous basilica, has left him puzzled. Built in the early 1900s by alleged miracle worker Saint André Bessette, the basilica attracts millions of visitors every year. "They keep his heart in a container filled with formaldehyde," Gil reports, disgusted. "It's supposed to heal the handicapped. The whole church is filled with crutches. Compare that to our ancestors who took a bite from the heart of a defeated enemy. That's how you get to his strength they thought."

Gil works in the Nation-Building Program at the Mohawk Council of Akwesasne (MCA). He and two colleagues have driven down to Montreal to discuss—over *steak frites* and a glass of wine—how we can collaborate on a philosophy workshop for members of their community during the fall of 2011. "What do you know about Mohawk culture?" Chief Brian David asks me. They laugh when I show them a photo from my childhood album dressed up as an Indian—from moccasins to feather headdress—in front of a wigwam in my parents' backyard. "The hero from my favorite Wild West novels," I explain. "Just the rifle and the horse are missing." "Never mind that rifles came from Europe and horses from Arabia," Brian replies. "At least the noble savage was a friendly fantasy." He even has plans to turn this fantasy into a business. "After five hundred years of colonial oppression we want to become a sovereign nation again, alongside Canada and the US. For that we need economic resources." So why not let tourists play Indians for a week: "Campfire, hunting, fishing, growing crops, sleeping in the Longhouse, song and dance—the whole package! Who cares that none of us lives like this anymore?"

The Mohawks are one of six nations that make up the Iroquois Confederacy, once the dominant power in what is now the northeastern United States and southeastern Canada. The Confederacy dates to the precolonial period. According to tradition it was founded by the "Great Peacemaker," a visionary prophet who turned a bunch of warring tribes into a powerful alliance based on firm moral-political principles—the "Great Law of Peace." The Confederacy and the Great Law define the political and cultural ideal that today's Iroquois nations strive to revive.[1]

One step in that direction is a self-governance agreement that Akwesasne is currently working out with the Canadian government. It is meant to supersede the Indian Act, which, in 1876, put an end to any form of sovereignty among Canada's Indigenous nations. The Indian Act was based on the premise that Indians cannot rule themselves and hence need the federal government to care for them—like parents looking after their children.[2] "But taking charge of our own affairs isn't going to be a walk in the park," Gil says. After their culture has been trampled on for so long, some of the most fundamental questions require new answers: how to reconcile modernity and tradition, what it means to live well, who should rule, and who counts as a Mohawk, to name a few. "And people in the community of course have different views on these issues," Brian explains. "So getting a discussion going is crucial to move things along. That's why we liked your idea of a philosophy workshop."

About twelve thousand Mohawks live in Akwesasne today. It's crisscrossed by five national and provincial borders: Canada, the United States, Quebec, Ontario, and New York. I get a taste of this fractured colonial geography on my way to the adult education center where the workshop takes place. From Quebec I cross over to Ontario, then pass the Canada-U.S. border (with the usual post-9/11 hassle: photo, fingerprints, fee, a cascade of unfriendly questions) just to return to another Quebec piece of the reserve after a ten-minute drive through New York. Angie Barnes, one of Gil's colleagues in the Nation-Building Program, tells me how the border police once pulled her over on the way to her father's funeral. "I really lost it," she says. "An athletic guy in uniform—I stared him down until he let me go."

On average fifteen members of the community participate in each of the six sessions of the workshop we undertake that fall. They bring a wide range of views and backgrounds to the discussion. The staff of the Nation-Building Program is usually there—besides Gil and Angie, Sarah Herne and Wendy Adams. Angie was also the first female grand chief of the MCA, the official governing body on the Canadian side of the reserve. Other regulars include Darren Bonaparte, an Akwesasne historian, who is working on restoring the community's cultural memory; Geraldine Jacobs, who is trying to rebuild her Mohawk identity after going through Canada's notorious residential school system, set up in the nineteenth century to "civilize" Indians; Jackie Mitchell, whose father is white and who has been a Mohawk on and off according to changing membership rules; Josh Sargent, a "professional rebel," who taught himself philosophy, politics, and economics and rejects the MCA as an instrument of the colonial power; Joyce King, a former editor of the *Indian Times* who now heads Akwesasne's Justice Department; and Tobi Mitchell, who works at the MCA's Aboriginal Rights and Research Office.

"Don't we have better things to do than discuss philosophy for four hours?" Tobi asks. "Well, isn't it important to replace false beliefs with true ones?" I reply. "Consider these claims: 'Indians are pagans and must be converted' or 'Indians are savages and must be civilized' or 'Indians are immature and cannot govern themselves.' Shouldn't we care to refute them?" I quote from a 1455 bull by Pope Nicholas V, in which the Catholic Church approved the colonial enterprise. Europe's Christian nations were given a free hand to "invade and subdue all pagans and other enemies of Christ," to "reduce their persons to perpetual slavery," to "appropriate their possessions and goods," and to "convert them to their profit."[3] Tobi remains skeptical: "Did the colonizers really do wrong because they had false beliefs or did they come up with false beliefs to justify their crimes?" "I think you'll find both," I reply. "Many Jesuits, for example, really thought they were saving souls by converting Indians." I concede though that right beliefs alone will not deter someone who wants to do wrong. "They need to be enforced. If it's wrong to take what's yours *and* laws are enforced that protect your property, then I won't take it even if I want to." I mention the Dominican friar Bartolomé de las Casas who, in the sixteenth century, described the atrocities of the Spanish *conquista* and argued that Indians, like Christians, are free men in the natural order and hence cannot be enslaved. "His defense became policy with the 'New Laws for the Good Treatment of the Indians' issued by Emperor Charles V."[4] Darren points out that the laws were not really applied. "True, their impact was limited. But does that mean that discussing these issues is futile?"

I propose a different way to motivate the discussion: "Take a proposal for building a new hydroelectric dam close to the reserve. You know it will generate revenue and jobs, but also contaminate the environment. Would you reject the proposal?" Gil offers another example of conflicting values: "Lots of people talk about sovereignty. But if you ask them if they're going to help fund public services that Canada now pays for—collecting garbage, paving roads, health centers, schools—there's much less excitement. So I ask them: what's sovereignty really worth to you?" Philosophy can help here, I suggest: "Getting clear on what you value most, identifying value conflicts, thinking about the conditions that allow you to live according to your values and so forth."

The hydroelectric dam example isn't just a thought experiment in Akwesasne, which straddles the St. Lawrence River. In the 1950s both the St. Lawrence Seaway—a key shipping route between the Atlantic and the Great Lakes—and the Moses-Saunders Power Dam were built. Both were joint ventures of Canada and the United States. "The difference with your example is that nobody asked for our opinion," Joyce remarks. Traditional farmlands were destroyed and Mohawk families relocated, but the worst was the heavy industry that came to the region.[5] "They dumped their toxic waste in our backyard," Joyce explains. "The pollution destroyed our traditional economy—hunting, fishing, and agriculture." Already in the 1980s pregnant women and children were advised to keep away from local fish altogether. "So do everyone's interests count equally?" I ask. "Or does the fact that lights go on and washing machines spin in New York and Montreal justify the damage the Power Dam did to Akwesasne?"

"Experiences like these help us make the case for the self-governance agreements," Gil explains. Many in the community have doubts about the moral integrity of their own leaders. "We still have memories of chiefs trading land for a barrel of whiskey. But how can we trust Canada to make decisions in our best interest?" That leads us to ask another important question: How can one ensure that leaders act in the best interest of the community?

"But we have a pretty clear idea about how to live, organize our community, choose our leaders," Sarah says. "So what do we need you for?" "I'm not here of course to teach you any of this," I reply. "What I mean by philosophy is just tools to think about these questions and help getting a discussion off the ground." "And why don't you do that in your own community? Do we need help more than they do?" Sarah wants to know. I mention the workshops I did with Hasidic Jews in New York and high school students in Brazil—two contexts tied to my own biography. "In principle I think everyone would benefit from these discussions. But in Akwesasne you can't avoid fundamental questions right now—about identity, justice, government, and so forth. So there's a greater sense of urgency than in other communities."

"I don't think we'd be inviting people like you if we felt more confident about what we believe," Jackie says. "So people who are very confident about their beliefs don't need to participate in these discussions?" I ask. "Imagine that at birth you were by accident switched in the hospital and brought up as a Canadian. Wouldn't you believe many things with great confidence that are very different from those you actually believe?"[6] Sarah protests: "Being a Mohawk is in our blood!" She mentions Mohawks who were adopted into white families and later desperately tried to find their biological parents. "So you're claiming that the core beliefs that make up our identity are innate, not learned?" I ask. "That's an interesting question."

But we may not even need to leave Akwesasne for this thought experiment. "Isn't the community divided along cultural-religious lines?" Some have returned to the ancestral Longhouse religion, others worship in the St. Regis Catholic Church or the Hogansburg Methodist Church. Still others belong to the Longhouse of Handsome Lake, the eighteenth-century reformer who tried to save tradition by adapting it to the colonial setting. "So," I go on, "you'd have the same effect if you switch two Mohawk babies across these divisions."

Today many reject Handsome Lake's reform as a corruption of authentic tradition. Sometimes the divisions pit parents against children. Angie tells how painful it was for her mother and grandmother—both practicing Catholics—when she decided to join the traditional Longhouse. "I felt torn for a long time. When I finally received my new Mohawk name—Tsioneratase—in a Longhouse ceremony it was a great relief." "Does that mean that traditionalists think Catholicism is wrong?" I ask. There's reluctance to admit this. "How can we judge others, if we haven't walked in their moccasins?" Sarah replies. But some participants are less shy to pass judgment. "I was an altar boy as a child," Gil tells, "but at some point things like the trinity, the incarnation, or the virgin birth just didn't make sense to me anymore."

I suggest distinguishing between having false beliefs and being responsible for them. "Take someone who lived before the Copernican revolution and believed that the earth is at the center of the universe. He was wrong, but we wouldn't blame him. So even if we're sure that the people we disagree with are wrong, we needn't hold them responsible for that."

Acknowledging deep disagreements poses another problem, as Joyce points out: "In our tradition, decisions about community issues are based on two principles: autonomy and consensus." People cannot be forced to endorse something they don't believe in. At the same time, the assumption is that at the end of the discussion a consensus will emerge. "Now our minds are one" is reiterated throughout the "Thanksgiving Address," a key text of the Iroquois cultural revival, in which gratitude is expressed to the different parts of the universe for sustaining the community. That's why traditional chiefs had to excel in speaking and arguing. "One of their main jobs was to get people to agree," Joyce explains.

"The consensus ideal is noble," Gil remarks. "But can we still live up to it? Remember the Casino Wars." He is alluding to one of the most traumatic memories from the recent past: the escalating conflict over gambling in the late 1980s in which two Mohawks died.[7] In a 1976 landmark decision the U.S. Supreme Court ruled that Indigenous self-government entails the right to run gambling operations. Since then hundreds of casinos were built on U.S. reservations—a multibillion-dollar business that radically changed Indigenous economies. On one of my trips to Akwesasne, Gil and I stop at the casino on the American side. It's the most impressive building on the reserve, with its own hotel and restaurants. Visitors can choose from sixteen hundred slot machines and dozens of table games. We lose twenty dollars at the roulette table and then win fifteen at a slot machine. The casino's logo shows two Indians paddling a canoe. The decoration includes sculptures of turtles, wolves, and bears, the totems of the three Mohawk clans. But is the casino really part of Mohawk culture as this symbolism suggests?

At first two groups faced off in the Casino Wars. One argued that the casino would be crucial to attaining sovereignty because it would generate jobs as well as revenues to fund community programs—education, health, and so forth. The other group opposed gambling for religious reasons (the followers of Handsome Lake, for example, consider gambling a sin) or out of concern that a casino economy would destroy the traditional Mohawk lifestyle based on hunting, fishing, and agriculture. They also feared gaming's corrupting lure (one workshop participant tells how the tunes of the slot machines, the spinning wheels, and the falling money follow her into her dreams). "Then a third group emerged," Angie explains: "the 'bingo chiefs' who got rich and claimed that nobody has a right to the money they made thanks to their entrepreneurial skills." With their big houses and fancy cars they became a new model of success that especially young people in the community find attractive. "But this wasn't part of our tradition," Angie says. "We used to put the community first, not the interests of the individual."

"Of course nobody wants a war," I reply. "But why not a debate?" All three groups can offer reasons for their views: the importance of sovereignty, the importance of preserving a traditional lifestyle, and the importance of rewarding industrious individuals. "Colonial history," I suggest, "has created divisions in the community along cultural, religious, and moral-political lines. Wouldn't you agree that one way to deal with them is by coming together for a discussion?"

"I don't think that's foreign to our tradition," Gil says. "Didn't our ancestors sit around the campfire and discuss the community's concerns? The workshop can help us to revive that." He also points to the wisdom embodied in the Mohawk tradition. "Take marriage for example: You must marry someone from another clan and then the husband moves in with the wife. Would a son take up arms against his father? No! It's a good way to preserve peace between the clans. To our ancestors these things were obvious. But we have to work hard to figure them out after so many years of cultural oppression."

"Making this wisdom explicit—doesn't that also help to defend it?" I ask. I mention Dale Turner, a member of the Temagami Nation, who is now a professor of government at Dartmouth. He has argued for the need of "Word-

Warriors"—Indigenous intellectuals who are steeped in traditional wisdom, but can also engage the cultural discourses of the dominant power and assert the rights of their communities.[8] "But why should we have to defend ourselves?" Joyce objects. "They don't justify their ways to us!" "You can also put a positive spin on it," I reply: "Teaching Mohawk wisdom to the world."

At the end of the meeting Joyce tells me about her recruitment for Marc Halberstadt's docu-comedy, *Cowjews and Indians: How Hitler Scared My Relatives and I Woke Up in an Iroquois Longhouse—Owing the Mohawks Rent.* A descendant of German Jews, Halberstadt goes to Germany to reclaim the property that the Nazis took from his family. Then it hits him that just as the Germans owe him, he owes the Indians to whose land his family escaped. So he decides to cut out the middleman. He accompanies a delegation of Indians (including Joyce) to Germany to request compensation from the German government. "My own grandparents fled to South America," I tell Joyce. "But I suppose, if Halberstadt owes you rent, so do I."

I moved to Canada for much less dramatic reasons—to take on a job at McGill University. Later I find out that McGill's main campus was built on the grounds of Hochelaga, one of the first Iroquois settlements that the French encountered when they arrived in Canada. Next to the main campus entrance I discover the Hochelaga Rock, placed there by Parks Canada to commemorate this settlement. It's so well hidden in the bushes that I had never seen it before. The whole city starts looking different to me—when I stroll across Place Jacques Cartier in the old town, for example, drive over the Champlain Bridge, or pass by Collège Jean-de-Brébeuf in my neighborhood. Cartier arrived in Canada in 1534, erected a cross on the shore, and declared the land the property of the king of France. Almost a century later Champlain, the "Father of New France," set up the French colonial administration. He defeated the Iroquois in a battle in 1609, kicking off a long history of sour French-Iroquois relations. Jean de Brébeuf was a Jesuit who came to New France in 1625 to save Indian souls. He was killed by the Iroquois in 1649, and the Catholic Church canonized him for his supposed martyrdom. Clearly the heroes in one nation's story can be the villains in another's.

Reviving Mohawk culture is seen as a key to self-determination. "Our culture has always been put down," Sarah says at the beginning of our next meeting, "from the Jesuits, who wanted to convert us, to the residential schools that were meant to 'kill the Indian' in us. We want to express ourselves in our language and live according to our traditions!" "But are traditions good only because they were handed down by our ancestors?" I ask. Our meeting happens to fall on Rosh Hashanah, the Jewish New Year. "Almost every Jew—my wife included—is praying in a synagogue today," I explain. "But I don't feel bound by these religious traditions." The workshop participants are surprised. "Of course we wouldn't blame an abolitionist for opposing slavery—even if his parents had no moral problem with slaves," Josh says. "So only good cultural institutions are worth preserving?" I ask. "We can see that in our own history," Darren points out. "The Great Law of Peace put an end to a lot of bad things that the Iroquois practiced."

"Assume you could turn back the wheel of history to the time before the Europeans got here. All the scars of colonial history would disappear, but also many other things you're now used to in day-to-day life—from smart-phones and cars to medical centers." Everyone agrees on turning back the wheel (though one participant admits that she would miss Lady Gaga). "Does that mean that you're not losing anything of value or only that you have more to win than to lose?" I ask. Here the answer is less clear. "What if you could have it both ways—if the Europeans had treated you with respect as trading partners? Didn't your ancestors trade beaver furs against pots, axes, blankets, and other European goods?" "Don't forget the whiskey!" Angie says. "Fine, but does making a wrong choice mean that you have to reject the products of other cultures altogether?"

"Let's not get stuck in a fantasy world of the past," Josh says. "Living like a Mohawk doesn't mean we must become hunters and fishermen again, grow corn, beans, and squash (the 'three sisters' of traditional Iroquois agriculture) and move back into the Longhouse. Why should our culture not evolve like other cultures?" He sees the Peacemaker as a great philosopher who tailored his message to the cultural level of the Iroquois in his time. "But the core teachings—peace, power, and righteousness—aren't tied to those historical circumstances." We look at justice as an example. "The Peacemaker says 'Don't take more of the catch than you need to sustain your family' and 'Leave enough of the catch for future generations.' So he's speaking to hunters and fishermen. But why can't we apply these principles to a monetary economy in the industrial age?" Josh wants to know.

"Can one always separate core from context though?" I ask. "What happens to a culture built around the virtues of hunters and warriors when you buy your steak in the supermarket and no longer compete for land with your old enemies who live on reserves just like you?"[9] "I think we'll always need courage in this messed up world," Josh replies (whose anticolonialist activism, as he proudly points out, got him on the U.S. government's No Fly List).

"Is the Iroquois concept of justice universal or does it only apply to the Iroquois?" I ask. Darren mentions the Two-Row Wampum belt, a key icon of Iroquois culture, with two parallel rows of purple wampum beads against a white background. "People interpret the two rows as a symbol of how nations should relate to each other: living peacefully side-by-side without meddling in each other's affairs. We live according to our values, others live according to theirs." Brian concurs: "Cultural diversity is a good thing as long as there's no interference." "But is diversity always good?" I reply. "A math teacher wouldn't be happy about diverse solutions to a mathematical problem. Do we really want diversity when it comes to justice, the right treatment of nature, and so forth?" Even the symbolism of the Two-Row Wampum belt seems to presuppose universal norms, I point out: "All nations have the right to live in peace and freely determine their affairs. How could one condemn the injustices of colonialism without recognizing these norms?"

And conversely, did the Iroquois always act according to these norms? "What about wars over territory and trade advantages?" I ask. "Or forcing defeated enemies to adopt Iroquois culture?" "Maybe there's a colonialist drive in human nature," Darren suggests. "So a Mohawk Columbus isn't inconceivable?" I reply. "The Iroquois flag flying over Paris and London?" "Don't get carried away," Angie replies, "fact is that it was the other way around."

Gil asks Josh whether he believes in progress, since he claimed that Mohawk culture can evolve. "Don't you?" Josh asks back. "Wasn't the Great Law progress? Or the abolition of slavery?" "Maybe these things weren't progress but going back to how things should be—like repairing something that broke," Gil counters. "Isn't that what happened to Tadodaho?" Darren asks. Tadodaho is the legendary opponent of the Peacemaker. He has a crooked body and snakes growing from his head that symbolize his evil character. The Peacemaker doesn't kill him but changes his mind through arguments, after which Tadodaho's body straightens and the snakes disappear. He is "repaired" as it were. Gil is skeptical about progress. "New things solve one problem, but create another. We get around faster by car, but we also grow fat. Or take the community elders. We always valued their advice. They could guide the young because they had a lot of life experience. But 'progress' threatens that conversation. What do they know about smartphones, laptops, Facebook, and so forth. So on many things, the young don't ask them for advice anymore." Joyce agrees with Gil: "From the residential schools to the St. Lawrence Seaway—'progress' has been a catastrophe for us."

"But you still have to navigate between the modern world and tradition," I reply. "So when is the core of Mohawk identity compromised? When you use guns instead of bows and arrows or move from the Longhouse into a one-family home? When you adopt Western dress or speak English instead of Mohawk? Or when you reject the Great Law of Peace and stop reciting the Thanksgiving Address?" Drawing the boundary isn't easy. "Even putting down bow and arrow and moving out of the Longhouse is tricky," Darren points out. "It means that our very names only make historical sense!" Both "Mohawk" and "Iroquois" are names imposed on them by others. In their own language, the Mohawks are "Kanienkehaka," which means "People of the Flint." And the Iroquois are "Haudenosaunee," "People of the Longhouse." "From the flint in our traditional territory the tips of arrows were made," Darren explains. "That's why it was important. And the Longhouse represented the alliance between the nations of the Confederacy."

Geraldine, who attended a residential school, says that some people look down on her because she doesn't speak

Mohawk. But others don't see why they should make the effort to learn it. "They ask: How is it going to pay off?" Gil explains. One participant says she's all for transmitting Mohawk culture. Yet she sends her own son to an American school outside the reserve. "I want to keep his options open." Of course boundary questions arise in other communities as well. "Ultraorthodox Jews claim that Reform Jews aren't really Jewish and vice versa. And my wife and I have been discussing for ages the pros and cons of sending our children to Jewish school." "The difference though is that our culture lies in shambles," Angie replies. "We have to rebuild it before we can choose."

Our next meeting is devoted to the question of how to live. I quote a passage from a captivity memoir by James Smith, an American soldier captured by the Mohawks in 1755. He describes an intriguing debate about the good life that he witnessed in the Mohawk community. While everyone agrees that a good life is both happy and God-pleasing, there is much disagreement on what that means. One group argues that since God has endowed us with natural desires, he must be pleased when we satisfy them. That, in turn, makes us happy. A second group objects that when we follow our natural desires, we often harm ourselves and others. Hence suppressing them is what pleases God and makes us happy. Finally, a third group proposes a middle position: satisfying our natural desires pleases God and makes us happy as long as we do no harm to ourselves and others.[10]

All workshop participants side with the last position. "But the main reason I'm bringing this up," I say, "is to show that discussing the good life was part of your tradition. So let's pick up on that and ask more generally: what makes a life go well or badly?" At first they don't want to buy into the distinction. "Are you saying that some lives are worth more than others?" Angie asks. "A lot of people in the community aren't doing well at all," Sarah explains. She mentions health and psychological problems, violence and crime. "Who are we to say that these lives are inferior?" "Perhaps one can distinguish between a life's quality—how well it goes—and its fundamental value or dignity," I suggest. "Then one can say that some lives go better than others, although they have the same value."

The problem is compounded by the sense that the mess many are in isn't self-made. "Would we have gotten into the gambling and smuggling business if the colonial powers hadn't taken away our land and destroyed our way of life?" Gil asks. "But once people saw that they could make easy money smuggling cigarettes and other stuff they got greedy." Akwesasne is indeed notorious for smuggling all sorts of things over the U.S.-Canadian border—from cigarettes and, more recently, ecstasy to illegal immigrants. That is also the only thing that is regularly picked up by the media—much to the dismay of the community. "For the world we're a bunch of smugglers," Tobi says, "even though most of us condemn smuggling just as much as everybody else."

"But isn't a mess you're not responsible for still a mess?" I reply. "Let's say you lose a leg in a car accident that you caused because you were driving drunk or that someone else caused who was driving drunk. In the second case it's not your fault, but you still have to live without the leg."

"If you deny that at least in some respects one life can be better than another—how can you explain to your children that they're better off working at the health center or environmental task force than making the big bucks through smuggling or gambling?" I remind them of our earlier discussion about the lavish lifestyle of bingo chiefs, who represent a new model of success in Akwesasne—especially in the eyes of the young. "So isn't it quite urgent to discuss how important money really is for living well?"

"Just the other day, three young men involved in smuggling were killed in a car crash after a police chase on the reserve," Gil mentions. "They were my son's age." "I would ask my children if they want to live in constant fear—fear of prison, fear of death," Wendy says. She asks me if I've seen the 2008 film *Frozen River* that is set in Akwesasne. The husband of one of the protagonists dies in a smuggling operation, her child is given into foster care, and she herself almost drowns driving illegal immigrants over the frozen St. Lawrence River. "And if one could somehow avoid these consequences?" I ask. I tell Plato's story of the "ring of Gyges" that allows its bearer to commit crimes without punishment.[11] "I think smuggling itself corrupts people," Wendy replies. "They have too much money and time on their hands, buy drugs, get addicted—their lives slowly fall apart."

What, then, does one need to live well? We come up with a list of obvious items: health, courage, intelligence, friends, money, and so forth. "But are these things good in themselves?" I ask. I show them a self-portrait of Samuel de Champlain during the 1609 battle against the Iroquois. Arrows are hailing down on him as he fires his arquebus and kills two Iroquois chiefs with one shot. "Can one deny that Champlain was courageous?" I ask. "Well, even if he was," Gil replies, "he used his courage for the wrong purpose!" Then I show them an iconic picture of a Mohawk warrior face-to-face with a Canadian soldier during the Oka crisis in 1990.[12] The crisis erupted when the Quebec town of Oka decided to expand a golf course and develop luxury housing on land that the Mohawk community of neighboring Kanesatake had been reclaiming for centuries. The standoff—first with the National Police of Quebec and later with the Canadian Army—lasted almost three months. The Mohawks eventually emerged victorious. "I suppose you'd say that here courage was used for a good purpose?" I ask. Everyone agrees. "So courage isn't in itself good, but only if it's used in the right way? What else do we need then?" "We need laws to guide us," Joyce suggests. "Any laws? Don't you have a long history of defying laws that you find unjust? The building projects in Oka, for example, were legal according to Canadian law." "Well, I was referring to the Great Law of Peace, not any laws," Joyce replies. "So laws that express wisdom? Are money, courage, health, intelligence and so forth only good if we use them wisely?" "I'm not sure it always has to be so cerebral," Sarah objects. "I left the church to join the Longhouse because it was more fun—singing and dancing instead of boring sermons!" "But can we really trust our emotions?" I reply. "Don't they often lead us in the wrong direction?"

"Who should govern?" is the question we discuss next. In fact, Akwesasne is the spot with the greatest number of governments on earth ("we should have an entry in the Guinness book of records," Angie says). As mentioned, it falls under two federal jurisdictions, Canada and the United States, and three provincial ones, Quebec, Ontario, and New York. Technically, the queen of England has the last say on the Canadian side. Add to this two governing bodies on the reserve: the Mohawk Council of Akwesasne that Canada recognizes, and its American counterpart, the St. Regis Mohawk Council. Finally, there is the Mohawk Nation Council of Chiefs and Clan Mothers, which the community sees as the only legitimate heir of traditional Mohawk governance, but which neither Canada nor the United States accepts.

The paternalist Indian Act of 1876 put the state in charge as guardian of Canada's Indigenous nations. The goal was to get Indians to "grow up" and then assimilate them into "civilized" society.[13] When the 1948 Universal Declaration of Human Rights stressed that "all human beings are born free and equal," this kind of disregard for freedom and equality became untenable. In 1969, Minister of Indian Affairs Jean Chrétien released a White Paper proposing to abolish the Indian Act. Indians should become regular citizens with the same rights and obligations as all Canadians. Like the English, French, Italians, Jews, Greeks, and so forth, they would be one cultural community among many contributing to Canada's "multicultural mosaic."[14]

Indigenous communities unanimously rejected Chrétien's proposal. "We have a very different idea of what freedom and equality mean," Gil explains. "Freedom means taking charge of our own affairs as a sovereign nation. And equality means that we establish a nation-to-nation relationship with the former colonial powers."

Akwesasne's self-governance agreements with Canada are considered an important step in this direction. So I'm surprised to learn how controversial they are in the community. "You know the battered wife syndrome?" Darren asks. "The colonial power abuses us again and again, but instead of leaving it we say it's our fault!" The heart of the problem is a structural one. The MCA is an elected council, modeled on a Western-style representative democracy. "But traditional Mohawk governance is a form of participatory democracy—bottom-up, not top-down," Darren explains. "So people reject the MCA as something imposed by the colonial power. Hardly anyone shows up for elections" (with a voter turnout of two to three hundred, the democratic legitimacy of the MCA is indeed a sham). "So why don't you get rid of the MCA?" I ask. "The catch is that the MCA gets all the cash from the federal government—seventy million dollars that fund everything from education to healthcare. It's also by far the biggest employer in town." Few are willing to make as big a sacrifice as Josh, who homeschools his children and opted out of the MCA's programs and benefits. "I refuse to get drawn into the colonial enterprise," he explains. "I agree with Josh that the MCA is a colonial instrument," Sarah says. "But I work for it because I have to put bread on the table." The Mohawk Nation Council of Chiefs and Clan Mothers, by contrast, enjoys wide support in the community ("you often can't get a spot at the Longhouse; up to six hundred people come out for the Midwinter Ceremony for example," Angie points out). But it cannot do much because Canada gives it no money. "It's a form of blackmail," Darren says. "If we're serious about self-governance, we'll lose our funding. If we want to keep our funding, power goes to the MCA that nobody believes in."

Tellingly, not one MCA chief came to the meeting, while several members of the Mohawk Nation Council are eager to make their voice heard. Howard Thompson, a traditional chief, wonders if the question "Who should govern?" does not miss the point from the outset: "If by 'govern' you mean some form of coercion—that's not part of our tradition," he explains. "So you're saying that the political ideal of the most-governed place on earth is no government at all?" I ask. He nods and laughs.

There is support for his claim in the *Jesuit Relations*—the annual reports that Jesuits in New France sent to Rome from the seventeenth century onward. Here is how Jean de Brébeuf described the role of chiefs in 1636: "The first rank is held by those who have acquired it by their intelligence, eloquence, magnificence, courage, and wise conduct. . . . These chiefs do not govern their subjects by means of command and absolute power, as they have no force at hand to compel them to do their duty. Their government is only civil, and they merely represent what is to be done for the good of the village or of the whole country. Beyond that, everyone does as they please."[15] The principle underlying this concept of governance is "the primacy of conscience," argues Taiaiake Alfred, a Mohawk intellectual from the Kahnawake reserve just outside of Montreal, who now teaches Indigenous governance at the University of Victoria. "Leaders rely on their persuasive abilities to achieve a consensus that respects the autonomy of individuals."[16]

"Have you seen the 1969 documentary *You Are on Indian Land*?" Howard asks me. "It's a good illustration of how we think." That year Akwesasne Mohawks blocked the Cornwall Bridge that connects the United States and Canada over the St. Lawrence River in protest against Canada's decision to prohibit the duty-free passage of personal goods across the border. Their right to do so, the

Mohawks argued, was established by the Jay Treaty of 1794. The spokesman of the protesters was Ernest Benedict, one of the most respected Mohawk leaders and educators. When the Canadian police officer in charge told him to call off the blockade, he explained that neither he nor anyone else had the power to do so: "Everyone must follow his own conscience," he said. The police officer was clearly baffled and asked again and again who was in command. He couldn't get his head around the idea that everyone could be his or her own master.

This participatory model may not work for a modern nation-state. But why shouldn't it work on a smaller scale—for example, in Indigenous communities? "It's also popular with the worldwide protest movements," Josh points out (Occupy Wall Street is just taking off at the time of our workshop; its organizers make a point of deciding on the basis of consensus, not hierarchy).

Traditionally the chiefs were not elected democratically but chosen by the "clan mothers," the women with the greatest authority in the community. "Women were in charge of bringing up the children," Gil explains. "So they knew best who had the qualities to serve as chief. Why should a democratic majority be better placed to make that decision?" The clan mothers not only hired the chiefs but could also fire them if they did not act in the best interest of the community or in accordance with the Great Law of Peace. Such was the power of women that Jesuit priest Joseph-François Lafitau described Mohawk society in the eighteenth century as a matriarchate:

> Nothing is more real than the women's superiority.... In them resides all the real authority: the lands, fields and all their harvest belong to them; they are the soul of the councils, the arbiters of peace and war;... they arrange the marriages; the children are under their authority; and the order of succession is founded on their blood. The men, on the contrary, are entirely isolated and limited to themselves.... And, although the chiefs are chosen among them, they are purely honorary. The Council of Elders which transacts all the business does not work for itself. It seems that they serve only to represent and aid the women in the matters in which decorum does not permit the latter to appear or act.[17]

"That's not true," Howard objects. "Men and women take on different responsibilities, but one isn't above the other." Many important decisions concerned hunting and war. "So it made sense that the chiefs were men." "But does it still make sense now?" I ask. "The division of political responsibilities was rooted in the division of labor between men and women at the time. But today men often help educating children and women often help putting food on the table. So why can't men become clan mothers and women chiefs?" "Maybe men and women shouldn't be mingling in each other's affairs," Howard replies. "So you're saying that the traditional division of labor is based on the different natures of men and women, not just socioeconomic circumstances?" We don't reach an agreement on this question.

I raise another related objection: both chiefs and clan mothers are hereditary titles. "Why wouldn't you fill these positions with the most competent candidate rather than with one from a certain blood line?" "It's not that simple," Howard explains. There is the "pine tree chief," who is chosen on the basis of merit alone. And if no appropriate candidate can be found, chiefs and clan mothers are chosen from other blood lines. "But you still may not appoint the most qualified person," I insist. "If there's an adequate candidate within the relevant blood line, but a much better one from outside it, don't you have to go with the merely adequate one?" "The truth is, we've been debating this a lot here—if and how blood and merit are related," Angie says.

It's clear, then, that for many in Akwesasne self-governance is more than just the transfer of power. "First of all we have to decolonize our minds," Josh says. "We have to restore who we are if we want to take charge of our affairs in a meaningful way, not just reproduce the colonial system." How would this "authentic" self-governance play out in the way the community is organized? For our final meeting I propose to look at two examples of what's at stake: membership and property. It's a sunny late-autumn afternoon, all the regulars are there, and I even spot some new faces in the room.

Who is a Mohawk? In the past the Indian Act determined the membership rules. Jackie, for example, was not a Mohawk at birth because her Mohawk mother had married a white man, which meant that both mother and children lost Indian status. By contrast, a Mohawk man marrying a white woman retained Indian status, as did his children. As the place of women in society at large changed, such gender discrimination became politically incorrect. In 1985 Bill C-31 revised the rules: all Indian spouses and their children in mixed couples retain Indian status. From then on Jackie was a Mohawk and able to return to Akwesasne. "Of course nobody consulted us!" Tobi says. "Suddenly lots of people moved to the reserve, but Canada didn't give us additional resources to absorb them." The deeper reason, though, for the reservations about Bill C-31 seems to be that these days Mohawk identity is often conceived in terms of race. ("Our connection to the land and the community—it's in our blood," one participant claims. "As you can see, no one is more racist than we," Josh comments wearily.) At any rate, taking charge of the membership code is seen as an important step toward self-determination. "The basic principle I was raised with is the opposite of Bill C-31," Angie explains. "No one in a mixed couple can stay: if you marry out, you move out!"

Many in Akwesasne agree with this principle. "But doesn't that conflict with respecting everyone's autonomy?" I ask. "If you fall in love with a white person, will you become 'star-crossed lovers' like Romeo and Juliet?" "I dated a couple of white guys," Sarah says, "but I never felt a real connection—different beliefs, different values." "And what if you had only two options: a Mohawk you know is a fool and a white man you know is a prince charming?" I insist. "I'd have a child with the Mohawk and then move in with the prince!" Angie responds, laughing.

A second objection I raise is that the restrictive membership code that Angie described may lack a historical foundation. According to the Great Law of Peace, "if any man or any nation outside the Five Nations shall obey the laws of the Great Peace and make known their disposition to the Chiefs of the Confederacy, they may trace the Roots to the Tree and if their minds are clean and they are obedient and promise to obey the wishes of the Confederate Council, they shall be welcomed to take shelter beneath the Tree of the Long Leaves."[18] Sarah disputes that a foreigner can become a full member of the Iroquois confederacy. "The text only promises hospitality and protection that could be revoked under certain conditions." "But doesn't 'tracing the Roots to the Tree' mean more?" I ask. Darren points out that the Tuscarora nation only joined the confederacy in 1722. "And no one disputes that they are Iroquois." Josh mentions the eighteenth-century Mohawk chief Joseph Brandt, one of the most distinguished Indigenous leaders. Both he and his sisters had white spouses. "Were they living in Akwesasne today, they'd receive an eviction notice!" Even more puzzling is the well-documented story of two English boys, John and Zachary Tarbell, from Groton, Massachusetts, who were captured and adopted by Mohawks from Kahnawake. "They underwent a conversion ritual, were brought up as

Mohawks, and eventually became chiefs," Darren tells. "And then they left Kahnawake and were among the founders of Akwesasne!" "There still are lots of Tarbells in the community," Josh points out. "They're descendants of the Tarbell brothers." Several participants doubt the story's authenticity. But Gil proposes an explanation: "In the past the Iroquois were strong and ruled over vast stretches of land; so they could afford welcoming foreigners. We can't do that anymore."

"But is the blood criterion the best way to decide who's in and who's out?" I ask. "Perhaps this is another part of the colonial legacy," Josh replies. "The colonial powers tied membership to blood and we've internalized it—against our own tradition!" Gil points out that members of other Indigenous communities can become residents in Akwesasne after a five-year probation period. "It's really the white man we don't want." He was himself married to a white woman with whom he has a son. "People in Akwesasne sure knew how to make us feel uncomfortable," he says. At a Thanksgiving dinner his mother asked the guests whether they preferred white or dark meat. "When my turn came she said: 'You I don't need to ask, we all know the color you prefer.'" Even if this kind of resentment may not be justified, Gil finds it understandable: "Given our history, who can blame us that we feel hostile towards the white man?"

"But isn't cultural identification a better criterion for membership?" I ask. Just recently the MCA passed a new regulation that allows only a person with two Mohawk parents to run for the office of chief. So neither Jackie nor Gil's son would qualify. "Why is someone with two Mohawk parents a better Mohawk than someone with one?" I ask. "If the 'full-blood' Mohawk has no interest in Mohawk culture and language, while the 'half-blood' Mohawk spares no effort to learn them—who is the better Mohawk?" Josh mentions Ray Fadden, who came to Akwesasne in the late 1930s. Together with Ernest Benedict he is a key figure in the twentieth-century revival of Mohawk culture. His ancestry, though, is Scottish, not Mohawk. "Only after marrying a Mohawk woman was he adopted into the community and made a member of the Wolf clan," Josh explains. "But who wants to deny that he was a Mohawk of the very first rank?"

Since John Locke, private property has been a cornerstone of Western liberal societies. And that's how things in modern-day Akwesasne are owned as well. But Plato argued that we will work toward the common good only if private property is abolished: if the farmland or the factory is no longer mine or yours but ours. Then we will use them in a way that benefits everyone. Aristotle replied that human nature just doesn't work that way: we only really care for things we own.[19] "The Mohawks traditionally were on Plato's side," Howard says. "The moose, fish, and crops, for example, or the materials for clothes and tools belonged to all and were divided up fairly. And there was no sense that the land had an owner. We benefited from it and thanked the Creator for his generosity." The lack of a Western concept of property became a problem when the Europeans came. "They thought: this land doesn't belong to anyone, so let's take it!" Gil explains. (Robert Cushman, one of the British pilgrims who came to the New World on the legendary Mayflower in 1620, writes that the land of the Indians "is spacious and void, and they are few and do but run over the grass, as do wild beasts." This is enough "to prove lawful our going thither to live.")[20]

These days much effort in Akwesasne is spent on reclaiming lost land. I tell them how earlier, on my way to our meeting, I stopped at a souvenir shop whose owner told me that a new Oka crisis was in the making. She pointed to the Longhouse just behind her shop: "They're having a crisis meeting. Roger, a member of the Warrior Society, was arrested by the police!" I learn that Roger led the repossession (or, in the words of the police, occupation) of eight acres of disputed land close to the casino that has gained value as a potential site for a new hotel. The Warrior Society is the most militant group in the struggle for sovereignty. As I pass by the location, a group of men sit defiantly around a fire next to a large sign of the Warrior Society. It reads, "The Great Law has definite functions for the War Chief and his men (Warrior Society). They are charged with the protection, defense and welfare of the people. These duties may take many forms: keeping the peace, teaching, public speaking, repossessing lost lands and human rights; and work of all useful kinds to promote the welfare of the people. Upholding the Great Law results in Peace, Righteousness, Power—a noble work entrusted to the care of the Warrior Society."

"We've never ceded the land," Gil says. "We only leased it to white farmers, but a few generations down the road they started thinking that they are the owners." He will join the protest against Roger's arrest tomorrow. "I grew up with him."

"Does the fight for land force you to adopt a concept of ownership that's alien to your tradition?" I ask. "We always have to talk in the language of the colonial power," Darren replies. "So if you could, would you get rid of these concepts and go back to collective ownership?" Josh shakes his head. "I wouldn't say, like Aristotle, that it's against human nature. Communism may have been the right thing for the primitive hunter-gatherer society we used to be. But in the industrial age, private property and trade offer a much stronger incentive to be creative and produce stuff. As I said the other day: as long as we're faithful to our principles, I don't see why Mohawk culture can't evolve." He also feels that people in Akwesasne are at times hypocritical. "They talk a lot about collective ownership; but if you dig a hole in their backyard they'll come out with a gun and send you running!" "Does private property trump everything?" I ask him. "Suppose you're a wealthy factory owner while your neighbor has been laid off and can no longer sustain himself. Shouldn't there be a social mechanism to transfer some of your wealth to him—as in modern welfare states? Or if the fertilizer you're using on your field contaminates your neighbor's drinking water—shouldn't it be prohibited?" In the Western tradition, I point out, there are moral arguments that justify the state's interference in such cases—for example, John Stuart Mill's "no-harm principle": You can do with your field what you like as long as you don't cause harm to others.[21] "Any form of coercive state interference," Josh replies, "goes against our principles of autonomy and consensus. That doesn't mean that you can let your neighbor starve or contaminate his water. But you must do the right thing because you want to; and if you don't, there must be a discussion until a consensus is reached." He lists many reasons to motivate someone to help out his neighbor: "It will make you feel good about yourself; you'll know that you can depend on others should you fall on hard times; it gives you a sense of security because your neighbor won't break into your house in desperation; and so forth. If people get the right education and grow up with good role models, I don't see why a consensus can't be reached in cases like these."

"So were our four-hour discussions a good use of your time?" I ask at the end of the workshop. "We don't seem to have reached any conclusions," Sarah says. "Yes," Gil replies, "but I feel we got greater clarity on what the issues involve. And a taste for looking at them from different angles." I concede that philosophical discussions are often inconclusive. "So at some point you'll have to make a decision on practical questions—which cultural traditions to revive, how to govern, how to define membership, and so forth. What philosophers would encourage you to do is to revise these decisions in the future if convincing new arguments emerge."

"I thought that four hours of philosophy in the evening would put me right to sleep," Geraldine says. "But I actually had fun. It's better than chasing after dreams that don't come true."

PART II

DIVERSITY AND DEBATE

When I was ten years old, my parents decided to move back from Germany to Brazil. What was return from exile for them (they had fled Brazil's military dictatorship in the 1960s) was exile for me. Until then my world had been Maria Veen, a little town in former West Germany where my father taught math at the local gymnasium. The 1970s was a good time to grow up there. My parents had made friends among the school's open-minded young teachers, who were part of Germany's first postwar generation, and I became friends with their children. From the sandbox to elementary school Maria Veen was home. Literally overnight this world turned into a small spot far away. In São Paulo, where my parents grew up, everything was different—from climate, language, and cuisine to etiquette, culture, and social class. Since my family was Brazilian, I did not have the buffer zone provided by communities of immigrants that normally allow some distance from the new culture. I was not used to being greeted with hugs and kisses and could not understand why it was polite to arrive a half hour late when we were invited to someone's home. The mother of one of my classmates spent hours in front of a crucifix imploring Christ to help his older brother get into law school. To cover all her bases, she instructed her maid to make offerings to Afro-Brazilian deities as well. Another classmate was driven to school by a private chauffeur and had two maids and a cook to attend to him in his family's villa, which, like a fortress, was surrounded by high walls covered with barbed wire, and sported an armed guard at the entrance gate. Among my most disconcerting discoveries was that nobody had heard of the heroes that shape every German boy's imagination: Winnetou, the noble chief of the Apaches, and Old Shatterhand, his white brother in arms—the protagonists of Karl May's popular Wild West novels; or Erich Kästner's Emil and his detective friends, pursuing the wicked bank robber Max Grundeis.[1] Instead I was introduced to the characters of Monteiro Lobato's *Sítio do Picapau Amarelo* (The farm of the yellow woodpecker), including Dona Benta and her two grandchildren: Lúcia, known by her nickname, Narizinho ("Little Nose" because of her turned-up nose), and her cousin, Pedrinho; Nastácia, their black servant and cook; and two talking puppets: the rag doll Emília (animated by Doctor Snail's "talking pills," which she had somehow ingested) and the Visconde de Sabugosa, an aristocratic, learned puppet made of corncob.

My response to this experience was to cling to all things German while putting down all things Brazilian—a kind of diaspora nationalism. I insisted on reading German books, kept writing letters back and forth with my former German classmates, and even insisted that my parents take us to a German restaurant (the *Juc Alemão*) once in a while, although we had never eaten German food at home. While having my world turned upside down was painful, it also forced me to assess the beliefs and values that until then I had taken for granted. Looking back, the ethnocentric biases of my teenaged judgments are, of course, embarrassing. Yet they were also a first clumsy attempt to defend a certain view of things and way of life.[2]

In the preface to this book, I mentioned a similar experience from more recent years: the inconclusive discussions about God's existence with Egyptian students in Cairo, prompted by our concern about how one should live. They wanted to save my soul from eternally burning in hell by converting me to Islam; I wanted to save them from wasting their real life for an illusory afterlife by converting them to the secular worldview I grew up with. As in Brazil, I came face-to-face with beliefs and values that I had adopted without reflection in a particular sociocultural context—from my atheism to my idea of a good life. The challenge by my Egyptian friends forced me to ask myself how well founded these views really were.

I also learned from our discussions that my views are widely contested. After we moved back to Germany for various reasons, I completed high school in 1990, in the middle of Germany's turbulent reunification (I ended my final exam in history by describing the newest political developments I had heard on the radio that same morning). For a few years after the breakdown of the Soviet bloc, many people, especially in the West, thought that soon the values and lifestyles of Western liberal democracies would be adopted all over the world.[3] Years later, the discussions with my Egyptian friends brought home that I'd better not hold my breath. And so did my subsequent discussions with Palestinians, Indonesians, Hasidic Jews, Brazilians, and Mohawks that I describe in the first part of this book. While we often regret the persistent disagreements on fundamental moral, religious, and philosophical questions, I want to argue here that these disagreements can be a good thing—to the extent we can make them fruitful for what I propose calling a "culture of debate." For the philosopher Charles Taylor, experiences like mine—of being displaced in Brazil or of engaging in disputes in Egypt—bring to light what he calls "the sources of the self": the beliefs and values embedded in a culture that shape our identity and the way we live.[4] Under normal circumstances these sources remain hidden and inarticulate. My claim is that we should welcome the disruptions that compel us to confront them.[5]

DEBATE AND TRUTH

Can we be sure that our beliefs about the world match how the world actually is, that our beliefs about what is right capture true moral norms, and that our subjective preferences match what is objectively in our best interest? If the truth is important to us, these are pressing questions. We might value the truth for different reasons: because we want to live a life that is good and doesn't just appear so; because we take knowing the truth to be an important component of a good life; because we consider living by the truth a moral obligation independent of any consequences; or because, like my Egyptian friends, we want to come closer to God, who is the Truth (*al-Ḥaqq* in Arabic, one of God's names in Islam).[6]

Of course we wouldn't hold our beliefs and values if we were not *convinced* that they are true. But that's no evidence that they are. Weren't my Egyptian friends just as convinced of their views as I was of mine? The seventeenth-century French philosopher Pierre Bayle put it this way: I am aware of "a great many others" who are "as worthy as I," yet disagree with me on many things.[7] Looking just at my own family over a few generations, the variety of moral, religious, and philosophical views held by siblings, parents, grandparents, and great-grandparents is striking: they include pious Jews and Catholics, slave-holding plantation owners and communists, Yoga enthusiasts and atheists. I disagree with them on many things, but can I be sure that I am always right and they always wrong? Many of our views, Bayle argues, are not based on "demonstrations," but on "probable reasons which do not appear so to other men."[8] Indeed, Bayle (who was raised a Protestant, converted to Catholicism, and then returned to Protestantism) points out that over time we even disagree with ourselves:

"Every man" experiences "his own proneness to error and sees . . . in growing older the falsehood of several things which he had believed to be true."[9] So how can we be sure that we will not revise our present beliefs in the future?

Or consider the bewildering diversity of beliefs and values, all held with great conviction, across different times and cultures. As Gil Terrance from the Mohawk Council in Akwesasne pointedly asked, "So who's the savage here?" Catholic Quebeckers who revere the heart of an alleged miracle worker on display in a container filled with formaldehyde at St. Joseph's Oratory in Montreal or Iroquois warriors who took a bite from the heart of a defeated enemy to absorb his courage?[10] Already in antiquity an anonymous contemporary of Socrates observed how much that "which cities and nations consider seemly and shameful" varies from one to the next:

> To Spartans, for example, it is seemly that girls should exercise naked or walk around bare-armed or without a tunic, but to Ionians this is shameful. And [in Sparta] it is seemly that boys should not learn arts or letters, but to Ionians it is shameful not to know all these things. . . . To Macedonians it appears to be seemly that girls should love and have intercourse with a man before marrying him, but shameful to do this once they are married. To Greeks both practices are shameful. The Thracians count it an adornment that their girls tattoo themselves, but in the eyes of everyone else tattoo-marks are a punishment

> for wrongdoers.... Massagetes cut up their parents and then eat them, and it seems to them an especially seemly form of entombment to be buried inside one's children; if a person did this in Greece he would be driven out of Greece and die a miserable death for doing things that are shameful and horrible.[11]

And this is the author's conclusion: "I think that if one were to order all mankind to bring together into a single pile all that each individual considered shameful, and then again to take from this pile what each thought seemly, nothing would be left."[12] If considerations such as these lead us to concede that our present convictions could be false, then we are *fallibilists.*[13] And if we are fallibilists, we can see why valuing the truth and valuing a culture of debate are related. According to fallibilists, we can never be absolutely certain that what we believe and value is right. At the same time, fallibilists assert the existence of objective norms in relation to which we can be wrong and to which we can get closer by critically examining our beliefs and values. To that end, in turn, a culture of debate offers an excellent setting. So one purpose of a culture of debate is to enable a *joint search for the truth.* Although our moral, religious, and philosophical views widely differ, we share the desire to get them right.

Of course we don't need to travel all the way to São Paulo or Cairo to subject our beliefs and values to critical scrutiny; in theory, we can do that from the armchair in our living room. In practice, however, we seem to need some sort of unsettling experience that confronts us with our fallibility, or, as al-Ghazālī puts it in his intellectual autobiography, *The Deliverance from Error*, something that breaks the "bonds of *taqlīd*"—the beliefs and values stemming from the contingent circumstances of our socialization. In chapter 3 we saw how in al-Ghazālī's own case, the bonds of *taqlīd* broke when he realized that he would have been just as fervent a Jew or Christian as he was a Muslim, had he been brought up in a Jewish or Christian community: "As I drew near the age of adolescence the bonds of mere authority [*taqlīd*] ceased to hold me and inherited beliefs lost their grip on me, for I saw that Christian children always grew up to be Christians, Jewish children to be Jews, and Muslim children to be Muslims."[14] Let me stress, however, that there is nothing necessarily *religious* about *taqlīd*. While contrasting secular citizens (who are allegedly intellectually independent) with religious believers (who allegedly follow the authority of faith) has become a commonplace in Western media discussions and among people raised in secular circles, my conversations with Egyptian students showed that I was at least as much subject to *taqlīd* as they were. Al-Ghazālī explains *taqlīd* as the authority of "parents and teachers," which we can restate more generally as all things other than good arguments that influence what we think and do: from media, fashion, and marketing to political rhetoric and religious ideology. The problem, in fact, is age-old. Already Socrates explained the need for his gadfly mission by comparing Athenian citizens to a noble but "sluggish" horse that "needed to be stirred up."[15] This experience, he admits, is not pleasant: "You might well be annoyed with me—as people are when they are aroused from a doze—and strike out at me. . . . You could easily kill me, and then sleep on for the rest of your days, unless the god, in his care for you, sent you someone else."[16] And yet, he argues, Athenians should reward him for his relentless efforts to free them from *taqlīd.* Interestingly, one of the earliest charges of *taqlīd* was directed against philosophers! Galen, the second-century Alexandrian doctor and philosopher, writes of Platonists, Aristotelians, Stoics, and Epicureans that they simply "name themselves after the sect in which they were brought up" because they "form admirations" for the school founders "without having learned their doctrines, and without having practiced the art of demonstration, by which they would be able to distinguish the false arguments from the true ones."[17] Galen, moreover, explicitly compares the *taqlīd* of philosophers to the *taqlīd* of Jews and Christians. His younger Alexandrian colleague, the Christian philosopher Origen (d. ca. 254), makes the same observation to turn the tables on Celsus, a pagan critic of Christianity, who accuses Christians of following religious authority rather than reason. This holds even more for Greek philosophers, Origen contends, who embrace their school doctrines without examination, unlike true Christian philosophers, who study the conflicting positions of the philosophical schools and endorse the one supported by the best arguments.[18]

Leaving ancient and modern polemics aside, the notion of *taqlīd* captures a general feature of human psychology: our disposition to internalize and conform to social and cultural norms.[19] If this is correct, and if we agree that *taqlīd* is an undesirable state to be in—at least when it comes to the core convictions that underlie our way of life and worldview—then we have a good reason for welcoming disagreements on fundamental moral, religious, and philosophical questions: namely as a means to break the bonds of *taqlīd*.[20] Our disagreements can play the role of the Socratic gadfly.

Particularly conducive to this end are debates *across boundaries*—cultural, religious, political, and so forth. When Jews discuss with Jews, Christians with Christians, secular citizens with secular citizens, Palestinians with Palestinians, Israelis with Israelis, or Mohawks with Mohawks, they will likely only scratch the surface of the historical, religious, and political narratives they were brought up with. If, on the other hand, we engage others who do not share our cultural narratives, we cannot rely on their authority, but are compelled to argue for our views—as I had to in my discussions with Egyptian students in Cairo. We must offer arguments that our interlocutors can understand because they are responsive to reasons, not because they belong to a particular cultural, religious, or political group. Consider a theological debate in the multireligious and multiethnic world of medieval Islam, described by the eleventh-century historian al-Humaydī:

> At the... meeting there were present not only people of various [Islamic] sects but also unbelievers, Magians, materialists, atheists, Jews, and Christians, in short unbelievers [i.e., non-Muslims] of all kinds. Each group had its own leader, whose task it was to defend its views.... One of the unbelievers rose and said to the assembly: we are meeting here for a debate [*munāthara*]; its conditions are known to all. You, Muslims, are not allowed to argue from your books and prophetic traditions since we deny both. Everybody, therefore, has to limit himself to rational arguments [*ḥujaj al-ʿaql*]. The whole assembly applauded these words.[21]

The principle at work is clear: the participants in the debate cannot appeal to their scriptures because none of them is recognized as authoritative by everyone. Instead they must convince each other by argument. So in a sense we can consider ourselves lucky to live at a time when societies are becoming increasingly heterogeneous and multicultural, and globalization forces us to interact across national, cultural, religious, and other boundaries. Due to technology, media, travel, economic ties, and so forth, there are no protected zones where we can avoid exposure to beliefs and values different from our own. In chapter 3, for example, we saw how the Internet allowed the outside world to break even into the Satmar community, traditionally one of the world's most secluded religious groups. Whether we like it or not, *in fact* we already find ourselves under pressure to justify what we think and do. The breaking of *taqlīd*, then, has become a ubiquitous experience in the modern world. Although it is often an unsettling, irritating, and painful experience, the benefits, I contend, outweigh the costs.

Of course diversity and disagreement on their own are not *sufficient* to bring about a culture of debate (otherwise the Middle East, the Balkans, and many other places would be philosophical debating clubs!). Instead they often generate frustration and resentment or, worse, erupt in violence (my Germanophilia in Brazil, for example, was largely fueled by resentment). The last thing we want is to get into fistfights about God's existence, the best way to live, the roles of husbands and wives, the education of children, and the many other things we disagree on. This is why we need a *culture* of debate—an institutional framework in which diversity and disagreement can be transformed into a joint search for the truth.

The last years of high school are a good place to lay the groundwork for such a culture. Attendance is obligatory in most countries, and the curriculum is not neutral—there's always something in the schools that people are unhappy with based on their moral, religious, and philosophical beliefs. High school is meant to equip students with the abilities they need to become productive citizens, and the curriculum includes subjects, such as evolution, that are more controversial in society than the subjects students would have to study to be able to engage difference and disagreement in a constructive manner.[22] So even if not all parents are delighted to see their children studying philosophy, this isn't a sufficient reason for excluding it from the curriculum. The classes I have in mind would focus on two things: first, conveying *techniques of debate*—basic logical and semantic tools that allow students to clarify their views and to make and respond to arguments (what Aristotelians called the *Organon*, the "tool kit" of the philosopher); and second, cultivating *virtues of debate*, most importantly valuing the truth more than winning an argument (that is, disciplining what Plato called *thymos*, the victory-loving part of the soul)[23] and trying one's best to understand the viewpoint of the opponent. Acquiring these techniques and developing these virtues can surely be done by high school students and would provide a viable foundation for a culture of debate.[24]

DEBATE OR COERCION?

But is a culture of debate really the right way to deal with diversity and disagreement? One could argue that if we cannot convince our opponent through arguments, we ought to resort to force. If conversion to Islam is indeed a condition for saving my soul, would my Egyptian friends be acting in my best interest by tolerating my stubborn refusal to see the truth? And conversely, if the afterlife really is just a religious illusion, would I be acting in their best interest by letting them persist in error? In his defense of intolerance, the fourth-century philosopher and Church Father Augustine argues that using force is an act of love and compassion: "If anyone were to see an enemy, delirious with dangerous fever, running headlong, would he not be returning evil for evil if he let him go, rather than if he took means to have him picked up and restrained? Yet he would then seem to the man himself most hateful and most hostile when he had proved himself most helpful and most considerate. But, when he recovered his health, his thanks would be lavish in proportion to his former feeling of injury at not being let alone."[25] Against this argument for coercion we can again appeal to fallibilism. What if the beliefs and values we intend to impose by force turn out to be wrong? Pierre Bayle's arguments that I cited above are, in fact, part of a fallibilist case for toleration. Fallibilism, then, offers us a reason both for critically scrutinizing our beliefs and values and for resisting the impulse to impose them on others—no matter how convinced we are of being right.[26] The medieval Jewish philosopher Maimonides, one of the best philosophers of his time, may serve as a cautionary tale. For Maimonides it was inconceivable that the picture of the world derived from Aristotle's cosmology and Ptolemy's astronomy could be wrong: the earth was at the center of the universe, while the sun, the planets, and the stars were embedded in celestial spheres that eternally circled around it, powered by God, the unmoved mover. Given the evidence and scientific theories available at his time, Maimonides was right to endorse this picture of the world. He was, however, so certain of it that he decided to legally enforce it as part of the Jewish law.[27] His intention was noble: Jews should honor the wisdom embodied in their religious tradition by holding sound beliefs about God and the world. However, not one of the doctrines that Maimonides tried to enforce by law survived the Copernican revolution!

Of course it doesn't follow from the fact that Maimonides was wrong or that beliefs and values vary widely across different times and cultures that it is *in principle* impossible to give conclusive answers to fundamental questions—from whether God exists to how we should live. Indeed, since Plato, philosophers have tried to find such answers: "reason," Plato argues, ought to apprehend "the first principle of all" and then deduce from it the true nature of everything.[28] Or consider Descartes's comparison of philosophy to a tree "whose roots are metaphysics, whose trunk is physics, and whose branches, emerging from the trunk, are all the other sciences, which may be reduced to the three principal ones, namely, medicine, mechanics and morality."[29] If the Cartesian program could be carried out, it would end all reasonable disagreement about God and the world, as well as about what belongs on the "pile of the seemly" and what on the "pile of the shameful," as the anonymous ancient author I cited earlier puts it. Everything would be known with the same certainty with which a mathematician knows that two plus two is four and a logician that bachelors are not married. We can find similar infallibilist projects if we turn to Spinoza and Leibniz, Descartes's fellow rationalists in the seventeenth century, or to the German system builders from Kant to Hegel. What is striking about these projects is how little their supposedly definitive results have in common. And when not only laymen but also experts widely disagree, we may have to make do with something less than absolute certainty.[30] Although fallibilists cannot expect a conclusive proof of fallibilism (being a fallibilist entails conceding that fallibilism may be wrong), surely it is a defensible position.

DEBATE AND GOD'S WISDOM

Making a case for fallibilism may not be much of a challenge if we are talking to a secular Western audience. Most participants in my workshops, however, had strong religious commitments, as did my Muslim friends in Cairo. They may well concede that *human* wisdom is fallible, but will often find it sacrilegious to claim the same for *divine* wisdom as revealed to Moses, for example, or Muhammad or the Great Peacemaker of the Iroquois. Indeed, they can argue that we need divine guidance, mediated through prophets, precisely because of our fallibility. And if we question the assumptions on which their views depend—for example, God's existence—they can reply that they accept these on faith, not argument. Does this mean that the fallibilist case for a culture of debate and for tolerating disagreement will not convince religious citizens?

A brief look at the history of religions shows that plenty of arguing was going on about how to understand

God's wisdom: within a religious tradition, with members of other religious traditions, and, more recently, with secular opponents. For one thing scriptures like the Bible or the Quran do not offer clear-cut doctrines and prescriptions. Deuteronomy, Isaiah, Job, and Ecclesiastes, for example, propose very different views about what it means to fulfill God's will and about why we are rewarded and punished. Moreover, these scriptures have been interpreted in many different ways in the history of the religious communities to which they gave rise. After losing his childhood faith based on the authority of parents and teachers, al-Ghazālī embarks on a quest to rebuild his religion. This leads him to examine the four main interpretations of Islam in his time, proposed by theologians, philosophers, Sufis, and Ismāʾīlis. All of them claim to represent true Islam. Does this diversity of interpretations not suggest that God's fallible interpreters cannot fully grasp his infinite wisdom, and that all interpretations should remain open to dispute and revision? Considerations such as these seem to inform the very structure of the Talmud, which, together with the Bible, is the foundational text of Judaism. The Talmud consists in a long series of mostly inconclusive debates between rabbis, in no systematic order, beginning with the question of how many stars must be visible for reciting the evening prayer, and ending with an intricate discussion of the impurity caused by menstruation. This structure clearly is not meant to promote pious submission to an authoritative body of laws and doctrines; instead it draws students into an open-ended, dialectical debate.[31] Consider, finally, the second-century Christian philosopher Origen of Alexandria, who required his students to study "all the writings of the ancient philosophers," admonishing them to be "neither biased in favor of one nation or philosophic doctrine, nor prejudiced against it, whether Greek or barbarian, but listening to all."[32] The purpose of this exercise was to confront the students with a range of conflicting views that would force them to think through on their own all the arguments on a given issue. In this way Origen wanted to ensure that their conclusions did justice to the wisdom he took to be embodied in Christianity. While this wisdom was infallible for him, he saw all human apprehensions of it as fallible approximations, open to revision in light of new and better arguments.[33]

While the rich history of disagreement and debate within a religious tradition—among theologians, mystics, philosophers, jurists, and so forth—may justify the claim that the *interpretations* of this religion are fallible, it doesn't justify the claim that the *religion itself* could be wrong. Can we be genuinely convinced of the truth of a religion and yet concede that we may be mistaken? Recall al-Ghazālī's account of how the bonds of *taqlīd* broke when he realized that, had he been brought up in a Jewish or Christian community, he would have been just as fervent a Jew or Christian as he was a Muslim. His beliefs and values, then, were derived from the contingent circumstances of his socialization. A religious believer might object that the community we are brought up in is not a matter of contingency, but rather the outcome of divine providence. Since members of other religious communities claim exactly the same, however, this belief, too, can plausibly be explained as the result of one's upbringing. Al-Ghazālī describes the quest triggered by this experience as follows:

> From my early youth, since I attained the age of puberty before I was twenty, until the present time when I am over fifty, I have ever recklessly launched out into the midst of these ocean depths... throwing aside all craven caution; I have poked into every dark recess, I have made an assault on every problem, I have plunged into every abyss, I have scrutinized the creed of every sect, I have tried to lay bare the inmost doctrines of every community. All this have I done that I might distinguish between true and false, between sound tradition and heretical innovation.[34]

According to al-Ghazālī, then, having trust in the truth of one's religion is no guarantee for it actually being true. This trust more likely shows that the bonds of *taqlīd* have not yet been broken. Of course none of this rules out the possibility of an independent proof that conclusively establishes the truth of a religion. And a believer can still claim that asking for a proof is wrongheaded from the outset, since religious truth can be disclosed only through faith. In this case, the fallibilist case for a culture of debate would fail. The two arguments I have sketched—based on the diversity of interpretations and from the contingency of beliefs and values—will thus not persuade *all* religious believers. They do, however, show that a culture of debate is compatible with the concept of divine wisdom.

AN ETHNOCENTRIC PROJECT?

It could be objected that the supposedly neutral space of reason and argument is not neutral at all, but an attempt to impose a secular, Western model of rationality on other cultural traditions. Hence, engaging diversity and disagreement through debate would be an ethnocentric project. Such a claim is based on a distorted picture of what these cultural traditions look like. In chapter 5, for example, we saw a model of grassroots democratic deliberation, as well as a sophisticated philosophical discussion about the good life in the Mohawk community. And Jews, Christians, and Muslims, as well as followers of Eastern religions, such as Hinduism and Buddhism, all developed rich philosophical literatures and traditions of debate. Al-Ghazālī, for one, stresses the importance for Muslims learning the Aristotelian art of demonstration (*burhān* in Arabic, translating the Greek *apodeixis*) to make sure that their religious beliefs never contradict "reason" (*ʿaql*). If a demonstrated doctrine conflicts with the literal sense of the Quran, the Quran must be reconciled with it through "interpretation" (*taʾ wīl*).[35] This solution for conflicts between reason and revelation was adopted in the twelfth century by the Muslim philosopher

Averroes and by the Jewish philosopher Maimonides.[36] It also contributed to naturalizing Aristotle's logic in the educational curriculum of the *madrasa*, the theological seminary in the Muslim world. As a consequence, theological discussions up to modern times were often conducted with the tools of Aristotelian logic.[37]

We've already heard about al-Ghazālī's quest to replace his childhood faith, based on the authority of parents and teachers, through knowledge. This is an ideal shared by a wide range of religious thinkers. Many medieval Jewish philosophers—including Saadia Gaon and Maimonides—endorse it. It also underlies the curriculum of the philosophical sciences, from logic to metaphysics, that the students of the Christian philosopher Origen had to master. Similarly Augustine (whose conversion to Christianity was prompted by studying the "books of the Platonists")[38] wrote at the beginning of his Christian career that philosophy best satisfies his "desire to apprehend the truth—not only as someone who has faith [*credens*], but also as someone who understands [*intelligens*]."[39]

This search for knowledge must by no means remain within the confines of one's own religious tradition. On account of his fallibilist commitments Pierre Bayle argues that if we want to come closer to God's wisdom, we must listen to anyone who might teach us something new or alert us to an error, even if he or she comes from as far as the (in Bayle's time) fabled *terre Australe*.[40]

Turning to antiquity and the Middle Ages, we've already seen how Origen kept his students on their toes by making them examine all the philosophical schools, "whether Greek or barbarian." Maimonides claims that we must learn "the truth from whoever says it."[41] When a student asks him, on one occasion, which works he should read for his philosophical education, Maimonides recommends Greek and Muslim authors, but not a single Jewish one.[42] Indeed, most canonical Jewish philosophers of the Middle Ages—from Saadya Gaon and Judah Halevi to Bahya ibn Paquda and Maimonides—studied the ideas of their Muslim neighbors so closely that we cannot properly understand them without taking this intellectual context into account.[43] When pious Jews today read the medieval classics they unwittingly renew the cultural bond with Islam. In chapter 3 we saw an interesting example of these intertwined worlds: the Sufi interpretation of a hadith in which the Prophet Muhammad contrasts the "smaller *jihād*," the *jihād* of the sword, with the "greater *jihād*," the *jihād* of the soul "against pleasure." A version of the hadith reappears in Hasidic literature of the eighteenth century through the intermediary of Bahya ibn Paquda's *Duties of the Heart*, a medieval Jewish account of the soul's ascent to God that was strongly influenced by Sufism.[44]

But are believers not somehow betraying their religion when they appropriate ideas from outside their own tradition? Recall the discussion with my Hasidic students in chapter 3: How, they asked, could medieval Jewish thinkers get away with interpreting the Torah in light of Sufism or Aristotelianism? Their approach to the truth of

Judaism, I suggested, is different from that of the contemporary ultraorthodox world: the medievals thought that they must interpret Judaism in light of the beliefs about God, nature, and the good that, upon careful reflection, they came to regard as true. If Judaism is true, they reasoned, it must agree with every true insight—even if it was stated by a Greek or Muslim. Today's ultraorthodox Jews, on the other hand, think that true Judaism must be sheltered from supposedly corrupting outside influences. In part this withdrawal—of which the Satmar community offers an extreme example—is a response to secular modernity, which threatens to obliterate traditional religion altogether. As one of my Hasidic students put it, "Our rabbis are not only building a fence around the Torah, but a cement wall!" We find similar forms of essentialism in other communities as well—Christian, Muslim, Hindu, and so forth.[45]

Let me illustrate the medieval approach through Averroes and Maimonides. Unlike Pascal, who famously opposed the God of the philosophers to the God of Abraham, Isaac, and Jacob, Averroes and Maimonides claim that the biblical God and the God of philosophy is one and the same. For them the main demonstration of God's existence is the physical proof that Aristotle worked out at the end of the *Physics* and in Book 12 of the *Metaphysics*. In a nutshell Aristotle argues that motion is eternal and that the instantiation of eternal motion in the universe are the celestial spheres, which eternally move stars and planets around the earth. Since the celestial spheres are finite bodies, they cannot contain the infinite force required to eternally keep moving. And since an infinite body is impossible, the spheres must be moved by an incorporeal mover—that is, God. Apprehending God in this way, Averroes and Maimonides argue, is the highest good for human beings, because the main component of a good life is intellectual perfection, which is acquired through knowledge of the natural order, culminating in knowledge of God. Leaving aside the technical details of Aristotle's proof, the important point for my purpose is that both Averroes and Maimonides claim that the first to establish God's existence in this way was not Aristotle, but Abraham![46] This is precisely the point on which Abraham broke with the star-worshipping idolaters of his time: they did not understand that the stars and planets require an incorporeal mover and thus took them to be the deity itself. Abraham is, of course, the founding father of both Judaism and Islam. By portraying Abraham as an accomplished philosopher, Averroes and Maimonides aim to embed at the very foundation of their religious tradition the beliefs about the world and the good that, upon careful reflection, they came to see as true. It is easy to see why they do this: they are philosophers, but Averroes is also a committed Muslim and Maimonides a committed Jew. Hence they interpret their religious tradition in light of their considered beliefs about the world and the good.

Arguably we should do the same: if we are genuinely committed to a religious or cultural tradition, then, to do justice to the truth we take this tradition to embody, we should interpret it in light of our considered beliefs. Doing so is indispensable for making a culture of debate work. One likely outcome of such a culture is that the beliefs we start out with will be refined and revised. So coming out of the debate, we will have to reinterpret our religious or cultural tradition accordingly. A culture of debate, then, is incompatible with an approach to religious traditions that seeks their truth in the *literal* meaning of the Bible, the Quran, the Vedas, and so forth, and takes that literal meaning to overrule our considered beliefs in cases where the two are in conflict. A culture of debate presupposes that religious and cultural traditions are open to interpretation and that interpretations, in turn, are open to revision.[47]

Besides intrinsic reasons for religious believers to embrace reason and argument (for example, the wish to replace faith with knowledge), there are also instrumental and circumstantial reasons. One is the internal diversity of religious traditions that I pointed out above: even if al-Ghazālī had wished to submit to religious authority, he would have had to choose between the competing interpretations of theologians, philosophers, Sufis, and Ismāʾīlis, who all claim to represent true Islam. How could he have made this choice without assessing the arguments supporting each interpretation? Or consider a Christian who must choose between Catholicism and Protestantism, and, within Protestantism, among the many denominations that claim to embody the legacy of the Reformation—from Calvinism to Unitarianism. Even if we assume, for the sake of argument, that we can make the right choice without deliberation, we would still face the problem that Plato raises in the *Meno* about true beliefs: as long as they are not "tied down" through arguments, they can easily "escape from a man's soul" if false beliefs are presented to him with sufficient persuasion.[48] Suppose al-Ghazālī had adopted the Sufi interpretation on mere faith (which is, in fact, the interpretation he eventually settles on). Would he not have discarded it if an eloquent theologian, philosopher, or Ismāʾīli had convinced him that it was false? Recall, moreover, that we live in a time in which globalization, migration, new technologies, and so forth make it nearly impossible to avoid exposure to beliefs and values different from our own. Under these circumstances, religious believers may want to "tie down" their beliefs and values even more to prevent them from escaping their soul. Of course this desire need not only be defensive. It can also be a desire to explain to the world why they hold these beliefs and values.

Let me finally stress that a culture of debate does not presuppose a Western-style liberal democracy as political framework. The only nonnegotiable "liberal" principle is freedom of expression. If citizens cannot say what they think without fear of punishment, a culture of debate is not possible. As far as I can see, however, no other liberal principles must be in place. The debates could, for example, take place in a monarchy or in a caste system, although this would limit the extent to which citizens could act on their considered political views.[49] Moreover, freedom of expression need not be derived from distinctly liberal premises—for example, as an aspect of our autonomy. It can also be grounded on the recognition of our fallibility.

My portrait of religious participants in a culture of debate is not meant to be neutral: they recognize their fallibility, reject the use of coercion, argue with members of their own and other communities, refine and revise their views, and reinterpret their religious tradition accordingly. This description obviously does not fit every religious believer. The fourteenth century Muslim scholar and jurist Ibn Taymiyya, for example, not only opposed certain philosophical views, but also rejected the use of logic as a Greek adulteration of what he considered the true Muslim faith.[50] Ibn Taymiyya became an important intellectual source for the purist Wahhabi (or Salafi) brand of Sunni Islam, the dominant form of Islam in Saudi Arabia, founded by Ibn ʿAbd al-Wahhab in the eighteenth century. Even the religious thinkers I have quoted—Origen, Augustine, al-Ghazālī, Maimonides, and so forth—do not fit my portrait in every respect. Yet once we discard the caricature of religion, drawn by critics of religion since the Enlightenment, as well as the essentialism of modern fundamentalists, it becomes clear that religious commitments can take many different forms. As I have pointed out, religious traditions are themselves diverse, shaped by competing interpretations (Ibn ʿAbd al-Wahhab's interpretation of Islam, for example, was vigorously criticized by his father and brother!). My aim here is not to pin down "true" Islam, Judaism, or some other religion, but to draw attention to the rich resources in these traditions that can motivate participation in a culture of debate. Since I am arguing for a certain approach to difference and disagreement, I want to show that it is possible to be a Muslim, Jew, Mohawk, and so forth in a way that is compatible with this approach. My portrait, then, is also normative, yet in a way that does not just betray ethnocentric prejudices, but can be supported from within many religious and cultural traditions.

DEBATE AND AUTONOMY

So far I've shown how valuing the truth and valuing a culture of debate can be related: if we want to get things right, concede that we may be wrong, and agree that we normally need a disruptive experience to break what al-Ghazālī calls *taqlīd*, then we should welcome debates across boundaries—religious, cultural, and so forth. I take valuing the truth—the desire to get things right about the world and the good—to be fairly universal. Of course not everyone who values the truth also values a culture of debate. Those who think they *have* the truth, for example, have no reason to join a culture of debate, conceived as a joint *search* for the truth.[51] However, as we have seen, the fallibilism required to get a culture of debate off the ground can be motivated from within a wide range of religious and cultural traditions.

In this section I want to briefly examine arguments for a culture of debate that appeal to a different value: the value of autonomy. Autonomy is often described as a distinctly "liberal" value that has little traction outside the modern West. If this were true, appealing to autonomy would be much more contentious than appealing to the truth. We could discuss the value of autonomy, but not assume it as the basis for a discussion across cultural, religious, and other boundaries.

At first view this perception of autonomy seems justified. Don't "we"—secular citizens of the West—cherish the freedom to choose: a career, a life partner, a way to worship, a political party, a school for our children, a pastime? And don't "they"—pious Jews, Christians, Muslims, and so forth—want to order their life according to God's will? On this side of the divide we are in charge, on the other side God is. Upon closer examination, however, the difference is less clear-cut. As I suggested above, *taqlīd* is a general feature of human psychology. Hence secular citizens, too, act on the beliefs adopted in the course of their socialization (as I did until being challenged by my Egyptian friends) and thus normally fail to live up to the ideal of autonomy. Conversely, submitting to God's will leaves considerable space for autonomous decisions: we need to evaluate and choose among different interpretations of a religion, and if, like al-Ghazālī, we experience the breaking of *taqlīd*, we also need to justify why we follow this religion rather than another. There are also other ways of bridging the gap that I don't want to pursue here, however. For my purpose it is sufficient if all sides—whatever their position on autonomy may be—take part in a culture of debate because of a shared desire to get things right. The meaning and value of autonomy can then become an object of discussion between them.

If we confine ourselves to Western liberal democracies, however, the ideal of autonomy clearly structures the individual, economic, and political spheres. This ideal encourages people to live by their own values, devise their own life plans, exchange goods on the free market, choose their political representatives, and so forth. Given this pervasiveness, it is worthwhile exploring why someone who values autonomy also has reason to value a culture of debate—even if outside the West such arguments may not be compelling. I will look at how such a case can be made based on the three major contemporary schools in Western moral philosophy: Kantianism, utilitarianism, and contractarianism.

For Kant only one thing has intrinsic moral value: an autonomous will.[52] Having an autonomous will means to know what is right and to want it for that reason, while resisting the inclination to do wrong. If we know that stealing is wrong, for example, and refrain from stealing for that reason—despite the perfect opportunity to pinch that much coveted watch—we are acting autonomously, according to Kant. However, doing what is right on account of authority—because our parents told us so, for example, or to avoid divine punishment—has no moral value for Kant. Being autonomous requires that we, as rational beings, give the law to ourselves, which means that we must use our own reason to determine what is right. We must, in other words, learn "to think for ourselves" (*selbst zu denken*).[53] This is a necessary but not a sufficient condition for autonomy since even if we think for ourselves rather than follow authority we may still make mistakes. Consider Kant's discussion with the French liberal intellectual Benjamin Constant about the duty to tell the truth.[54] Kant holds that we must be truthful under all circumstances, while Constant argues that sometimes it is justified to lie—for example, if a murderer knocks on our door and asks for a friend we are hiding. For Kant we act morally if we tell the truth because we know that lying is wrong, but not if we simply follow the biblical prohibition to lie (see Exodus 20:16) or some other authority. Constant, on the other hand, clearly thought about the issue for himself, yet reached—at least from Kant's perspective—the wrong conclusion. He thus is a "self-thinker" (*Selbstdenker*) without being autonomous. At the same time he can become autonomous—for example, by correcting his mistake in light of new arguments. A culture of debate, in turn, is a means to promote self-thinking, since Kant, too, is aware of the problem of *taqlīd*: "It is because of laziness and cowardice that so great a part of humankind . . . gladly remains minors [*unmündig*] for life, and that it becomes so easy for others to set themselves up as their guardians. It is so comfortable to be a minor! If I have a book that understands for me, a priest who has a conscience for me . . . and so forth, I need not trouble myself at all."[55] In order to break *taqlīd*, Kant recommends granting freedom of thought and expression—that is, the freedom to use "one's reason in all matters."[56] Kant hopes that the disagreements to which this freedom gives rise will compel citizens to think for themselves about the issues at stake. So a Kantian has reason to endorse a culture of debate: as a means to promote self-thinking, which, in turn, is a necessary condition for autonomy in Kant's sense.

The most sustained case for linking autonomy and a culture of debate was made on utilitarian grounds by John Stuart Mill. Mill's concept of autonomy is closely related to the idea of self-realization and thus is very different from Kant's. For Mill "individuality"—the development of our particular set of strengths and talents—is a key component of well-being.[57] Since our strengths and talents widely differ, we need the freedom to develop a life plan that allows us to realize our individuality while being compatible with the freedom of our fellow citizens. To this end, in turn, we need freedom of thought and expression—the freedom to think about and discuss different life plans in order to discover the one that truly suits us. Mill, too, is greatly concerned about *taqlīd*—"the magical influence of custom" that shapes our feelings of right and wrong and that we mistakenly take to capture objective norms.[58] Like al-Ghazālī, Mill stresses that our beliefs and values normally stem from the contingent circumstances of our socialization: "the same causes which make [a person] a Churchman in London, would have made him a Buddhist or Confucian in Pekin."[59] The informal power by which society "enslaves the soul" is the "tyranny of the majority," according to Mill.[60] As much as we need protection against the arbitrary power of rulers, we also need protection "against the tendency of society to impose, by other means than civil penalties, its own ideas and practices as rules of conduct . . . to fetter the development, and, if possible, prevent the formation, of any individuality not in harmony with its ways, and compel all characters to fashion themselves upon the model of its own."[61] Mill recommends a vigorous culture of debate to counteract the conformism that makes the "tyranny of the majority" possible and that prevents us from conceiving the individual life plan on which our well-being depends. Being exposed to disagreement, he argues, is a means to "break" the "yoke of authority."[62] The main reason for taking part in a culture of debate is that our beliefs about the world and about the good may turn out to be false, in which case they prevent us from realizing ourselves. Note, however, that Mill's case for a culture of debate does not depend on fallibilism. Even if the beliefs we adopt in the course of our socialization were indubitably true, we would still greatly benefit from defending them in a debate. For one thing Mill shares Plato's concern in the *Meno*: "beliefs not grounded on conviction are apt to give way before the slightest semblance of an argument."[63] And if a true belief "is not fully, frequently and fearlessly discussed, it will be held as a dead dogma, not a living truth."[64] So even the prospect of universal agreement (that some people consider a messianic promise), has distinctive drawbacks, according to Mill. Should such an agreement come true, "I would like to see the teachers of mankind endeavoring to provide a substitute for [genuine disagreement], some contrivance for making the difficulties of the question as present to the learner's consciousness, as if they were pressed upon him by a dissentient champion, eager for his conversion."[65]

A case for linking autonomy and a culture of debate can also be made from the social contract position advocated by John Rawls. Consider free and equal citizens negotiating principles of justice for their community. To model freedom and equality, Rawls proposes the "original position," where citizens negotiate behind a "veil of ignorance": the negotiating parties know nothing about their contingent empirical selves—their natural strengths and weaknesses, social positions, or moral, religious, and philosophical views. As a consequence, Rawls argues, they will agree on principles of justice that are acceptable to all citizens in whatever contingent circumstances they find themselves.[66] We may, for example, not be interested in granting freedom of conscience if we are part of the majority religion endorsed by the state. But we will obviously oppose religious coercion if we are part of a dissenting minority. Since behind the veil of ignorance we don't know to which group we belong, we opt for freedom of conscience. Similarly, we may not be interested in fair profit-sharing schemes if we are the owner of a factory. But if we don't know whether we are the owner or a worker on the assembly line, we will opt for fair distribution. Behind the veil of ignorance, Rawls concludes, citizens will agree on principles for distributing goods and burdens that reflect their freedom and equality.

There are two main things citizens will try to ensure for themselves, according to Rawls: rights and freedoms that allow them to devise their own life plans without outside interference, and the greatest possible share of resources that allow them to realize these life plans.[67] Unlike Kant and Mill, however, Rawls does not consider the problem of *taqlīd*. So he isn't concerned about the fact that, even if citizens have the rights and the resources to live as they wish, this is not sufficient to ensure their freedom. As we saw above, they will likely follow the authority of books and priests, as Kant puts it, or, in Mill's words, submit to the tyranny of the majority. Would citizens in Rawls's original position strive to institute a culture of debate to break the bonds of *taqlīd*? Although they know nothing about their empirical selves, they do know uncontroversial common sense and scientific facts, and take them into account in their deliberations. These facts arguably include the following: that we tend to live unexamined rather than examined lives, that our beliefs have a significant influence on how we live, and that some beliefs are more conducive to a flourishing life than others.[68] Since a liberal democracy, according to Rawls, gives rise to many different moral, religious, and philosophical views, we cannot know behind the veil of ignorance what the beliefs are that we will be brought up in—whether we will be born into a progressive or conservative family, a secular, a Hasidic, or a pious Muslim family, a family that values money and status symbols greatly, or one that stresses the importance of ethics and education. We do know, on the other hand, that we are often convinced that the beliefs we were brought up in are true and that we lack interest in subjecting them to critical scrutiny. So my claim is that citizens behind the veil of ignorance would chose to institute a culture of debate to compel them to reflect on the beliefs they adopted in the course of their socialization.

It is clear, then, that valuing autonomy and valuing a culture of debate can be related in many ways. A culture of debate would, above all, provide a space for critically thinking about moral norms, individual life plans, economic choices and political decisions, thus strengthening autonomy on both the individual and communal levels. It would, in other words, give us the tools to live up to the ideal of autonomy instead of following *taqlīd*—the authority of parents, teachers, and other social influences, from media, fashion, and marketing to political rhetoric and religious ideology. I take this to be a *supporting argument* for a culture of debate. The case for such a culture does not depend on it, but becomes stronger for those who consider autonomy a key individual and social value.

DEBATE OR MULTICULTURALISM?

If we can transform the disagreements arising from diversity into a culture of debate, they cease to be a threat to social peace. I now live in Montreal, one of the world's most multicultural cities. When a couple of years ago I had to see a doctor, the receptionist was from China, in the waiting room I sat between a Hasidic Jew and a secular Québécois couple, the doctor who attended me was from Iran, and the nurse was from Haiti. This was an impressive example of how Canadians, despite their deep moral, religious, and philosophical differences, can work together to provide the basic goods and services that we all need irrespective of our way of life and worldview. But while I certainly did not want to get into a shouting match about God's existence in the waiting room, or wait for treatment until everyone had agreed on how to live, I see no reason why we should ignore our differences altogether instead of making them productive for a culture of debate.

When I moved to Montreal in 2000, I was excited to be living in such a multicultural city. I expected to find a vibrant intellectual culture reflecting the many different and conflicting beliefs and values of Montreal's citizens. But it soon became clear to me that for the most part these differences are not articulated. Sometimes they erupt by accident. In my neighborhood, for example, there is a Yeshiva (a religious academy where orthodox Jews study the Talmud) across the street from the YMCA. The location allows Yeshiva students to watch barely clad men and women exercising in the gym—an unwelcome distraction from their Talmudic discussions that prompted the rabbis to submit a request to the YMCA to put up curtains. The request was met with outrage by the YMCA's secular users: "How dare these religious Jews try to impose their standards of decency on us?" The little skirmish offered a rare glimpse into the deep rift between the moral, religious, and philosophical views of citizens living side by side in the same Montreal neighborhood.

Was I right to be disappointed about the lack of critical engagement that characterizes Canadian multiculturalism? Should we indeed be asking fellow citizens to give reasons for the moral, religious, and philosophical views they hold? Does tolerance not require a respect for difference that is undermined by a culture of debate where we explicitly address our disagreements? Why would I want others to meddle in my affairs? Some advocates of multiculturalism ask us to celebrate, rather than just tolerate diversity, as if our differences were no reason for disagreement in the first place, but something good and beautiful—elements of a multicultural "mosaic." To be sure, many Francophone Quebeckers have reservations about multiculturalism too. They prefer French laïcité. Our moral, religious, and philosophical convictions shouldn't leave the private sphere, they argue: you are a *citoyen* in public and a Jew, Christian, or Muslim at home. What advocates of multiculturalism and laïcité have in common is that they try to remove our reasons for objecting to beliefs and values we do not share—the former try to remove them altogether, the latter try to at least keep them out of sight.

We can now see that a culture of debate represents something like a middle way between war and peace on the conceptual map of approaches to diversity: it is opposed to coercion, whose advocates argue that we should *interfere* with beliefs and values that we object to. And it is opposed to laïcité and multiculturalism, whose advocates argue either that we should *disregard* or that we should *equally* value beliefs and values that differ from our own. I have already outlined an argument for choosing debate over coercion. Let me now address the challenges of laïcité and multiculturalism. If the reason for privatizing moral, religious, and philosophical views is *political*—that is, preserving social peace—that privatization would be *unnecessary* as long as we can transform our disagreements into a culture of debate. It would, moreover, be *undesirable* if we value a culture of debate—because we value the truth or autonomy (or both). The concept of a multicultural mosaic, however, entails a stronger claim: that diversity is something intrinsically good.[69] The policy goals of the 1988 Canadian Multiculturalism Act, for example, include "fostering the recognition and appreciation of the diverse cultures of Canadian society and promoting the reflection and the evolving expressions of those cultures."[70] In some ways diversity is arguably enriching: we can choose between Indian and Chinese for dinner, listen to klezmer, bossa nova, or jazz, go to yoga classes, or practice tai chi. But beyond this, I find it impossible to value diversity. When I think of my five-year-old daughter, for example, I do not want her to grow up in an orthodox Jewish, Christian, or Muslim family, or, for that matter, in a secular family in which the idea of femininity is shaped by Barbie dolls and Louis

Vuitton bags. I have a clear idea of what I want to convey to her: a secular outlook on life, the value of education and ethics, open-mindedness, and curiosity for other cultures. And I want to convey these beliefs and values to her because I think that they are *superior*, not because I happen to hold them while those held by others are different but just as good. Someone may well object that this is an *ethnocentric* attitude. I am declaring *my* values to be *universal* values, although in fact they just reflect a contingent set of circumstances—my race, class, gender, education, and so forth. This may well be true (my list is certainly quite conventional for a liberal academic). Of course the fact that beliefs and values are held within a particular context does not itself invalidate them. My aim here, however, is not to defend what I believe. Surely Jews, Christians, Muslims, as well as members of many other religious or cultural communities would not want their children to be brought up in my family either. My point is simply that if we take ourselves seriously, we must be convinced that what we believe is true. When, back in Cairo, my Muslim friends and I discussed God's existence and how one should live, we meant our claims to be universally valid. In general we take the reasons we have for holding our beliefs and values to be reasons for everyone to hold these beliefs and values. This doesn't mean that we cannot be wrong about some, many, or even all things we believe. However, conceding that we may be wrong does not require us to give up the conviction that, in fact, we are right. It requires us only to recognize our fallibility, for which, as we saw, we have good reasons. If we are fallibilists, taking ourselves seriously does not rule out respect for the beliefs and values of those we disagree with: out of respect for them we will carefully examine their beliefs and values on the assumption that we may be wrong and they may be right. The attitude I endorse, then, can be described as *critical ethnocentrism.*

It is, moreover, unclear what proponents of multiculturalism mean when they ask us to recognize and appreciate other cultures, since easy-to-grasp monolithic cultural identities do not exist. As we've seen, cultural and religious traditions are diverse and contested. Orthodox Jewish men, for example, praise God every day in the morning prayer for not having been created a gentile or a woman, while liberal Jews purged the liturgy from elements they consider chauvinistic or sexist. Or recall the many divisions and controversies in the Mohawk community in Akwesasne that we saw in chapter 5.

A more important objection can be raised against the relativism that proponents of multiculturalism often appeal to: since values widely differ across cultures, they argue, no universal values exist. Hence we must equally recognize whatever values an individual or cultural group chooses to live by. Both steps of the argument are fallacious, but the second is especially problematic: if there are no universal values, then there cannot be a universal obligation of recognition.[71] In fact, many cultural groups do *not* value difference. We just saw one example: Orthodox Jewish men praise God for not having been created a gentile or a woman. The relativist argument can, moreover, be criticized on phenomenological grounds: things do not acquire value because a person or cultural group *chooses* to value them. If a young man decides to become a poet rather than studying law, or if a young woman opts for a pious Muslim rather than a secular lifestyle, they are choosing between values that exist independently of their preferences, and these values can be understood and debated, at a minimum, within the culture in which they are embedded.[72]

The popularity of relativism—most notably during the last decades of the twentieth century—is less due to its philosophical merits than to the legitimate discontent with ethnocentrism and its consequences.[73] These consequences include, for example, the atrocities—from colonialism to fascism—committed by Europeans in the name of supposedly universal norms, or the discrimination of women, blacks, gays, and other groups in the name of a supposedly objective concept of normality defined by white, able-bodied, heterosexual men. Unmasking the ethnocentric character of these norms and demolishing the moral certitudes that they were tied to is certainly a salutary process that has been championed by cultural anthropologists and their philosophical allies. While this critique of ethnocentrism has failed to justify relativism, it has significantly contributed to creating the intellectual space in which a culture of debate, based on a cautious and critical ethnocentrism, can unfold.

While a culture of debate may be a better way of dealing with diversity than multiculturalism, it faces a number of additional challenges that I can only sketch, but not fully address, in this chapter. I argued that relativism cannot ground a universal obligation to value diversity, and that our preferences presuppose rather than constitute values. This does not entail, however, that relativism is false. It remains quite possible that no universal norms exist: that what is right in one culture is wrong in another. The relativist can, in fact, point to the same evidence as the fallibilist: the great diversity of beliefs and values held with deep conviction across different times and cultures.[74] This evidence can also bolster the case of skeptics who deny that we can attain knowledge of what is right altogether. Recall the long list of practices considered seemly in one Greek city but shameful in another. This diversity can serve the fallibilist to remind us that our beliefs about the seemly and the shameful may be wrong, although we are genuinely convinced that they are right. But it can also serve the relativist who argues that standards of seemliness and shamefulness are valid only in a particular context, or the skeptic who argues that we cannot know what is seemly or shameful at all. If either relativism or skepticism were true, there would be no point in a culture of debate. We would be wasting our time if we could not get closer to the truth by critically examining our beliefs and values.

This does not mean that we can endorse a culture of debate only if we are committed to a one-size-fits-all view: that there is only one right way to live that we must first discover through debate and then universally agree on. A culture of debate is compatible with more or less robust forms of pluralism. Thus the basic elements of a flourishing life may be universal, yet realized in different ways in different contexts. Having friends, for example, is arguably a component of every good life, but the way friendship is cultivated varies widely.[75] Or there may be substantially different ways of living a good life. One person, for example, cannot have all the virtues of both a mother and a nun.[76] Endorsing a culture of debate requires only holding that not all ways of life are good, that how we live depends to some extent on our beliefs and values, and that we can improve our beliefs and values by critically examining them.

A culture of debate, then, presupposes the possibility of progress, something many find plausible not only in the sciences, but also with respect to moral values. A society without slavery, for example, seems objectively better than one in which slavery is practiced. In chapter 4 we saw Brazilian students in Salvador, most of whom had slaves among their ancestors, reject Christian justifications of slavery. But in chapter 5 we also saw how problematic the notion of progress is—from the perspective of Indigenous communities, for example, whose culture was denigrated as "primitive" and "unenlightened" by European colonizers. In general, narratives of progress that became popular in the eighteenth and nineteenth centuries played an important role in the justification of colonialism.[77] These narratives mostly lost their credibility after the catastrophes of the twentieth century.[78] But this does not mean that we must give up on a concept of progress altogether. For one thing the fallibilist allows that what is considered progress can always be contested. Moreover, progress need not be *linear*. It can be achieved at different times and in different places. And these achievements, in turn, may be lost and recovered under changing circumstances. Finally, if flourishing lives can substantially differ, multiple narratives of progress are possible. With due caution, then, we can retain a notion of progress, without which a culture of debate would make little sense.

PHILOSOPHY AND SOCIETY

As Plato noted, the claim that philosophy should be at the center of our individual and communal lives risks being washed away by a wave of laughter.[79] One aim of this book is to convince readers that joining a philosophical discussion is not ridiculous. Let me stress, however, that this is *not* a Platonic project where philosophers climb out of the cave, firmly grasp the truth, and then return to the darkness to enlighten nonphilosophers.[80] I surely have no definitive answers (nor, for that matter, do I know any philosophers who do). But consider again the contexts in which the workshops described in the book's first part took place. Each of them gave rise to fundamental questions: moral questions arising from the Israeli-Palestinian conflict, political questions about the compatibility of Islam with democracy and religious pluralism in Indonesia, questions about truth, religion, and education that my Hasidic students in New York were grappling with, questions about social justice in Brazil, questions about culture, identity, and good governance in the Mohawk community in Akwesasne, as well as more general questions, shared by many of my interlocutors, about reason, religion, autonomy, authority, and so forth. The essays in the first part of the book showed how philosophical tools can be useful here: to articulate these questions more clearly and to explore and refine answers to them.

Plato is deeply pessimistic about the possibility of democratizing philosophy. Was Socrates not executed for trying to turn all citizens into philosophers? Athenians did not thank him for guiding them to the examined life, but accused him of spreading moral corruption and atheism. And Plato concurs: Socrates failed because most citizens are not philosophers. To make them question the beliefs and values they were brought up with isn't useful because they cannot replace them with examined ones. So, as far as Plato is concerned, Socrates ended up pushing them into nihilism.[81] I wonder, though, why Plato didn't consider the possibility of training citizens in dialectic debate from early on. Wouldn't they have reacted differently to Socrates?

Plato's pessimism about the cave dwellers has a contemporary counterpart. Many theories held in intellectual circles these days consider our beliefs and values to be symptoms of something else that we are not aware of, but that determines what we think. A Marxist, for example, may dismiss my discussion with Muslim students as the clash between religious and bourgeois ideologies; both are functions of a social order in which one group exploits another. A Nietzschean may dismiss it as a disguise of the fight for domination, and a Freudian as a manifestation of suppressed desires.[82] If these theories were true, debates would resemble a puppet show, with the economic infrastructure, the will to power, and the unconscious as invisible puppeteers. This can lead to a form of elitism that shares some features with Plato's: the intellectual who has insight into the truth—into the real nature of things underlying the world of appearances—stands apart from the common people, entrapped in false consciousness. Some members of the Neo-Marxist Frankfurt School, for example, take liberal democracies to be camouflaged totalitarian states in which subtle forms of indoctrination subvert the freedom that the citizens think they have. Freedom of thought and expression, democratic elections, an independent press, and so forth are all a sham on this view.[83] Unlike the beliefs of Plato, however, such theories often do not consider the majority of human beings to be cave dwellers *by nature.* They are captives of a system that can be replaced—for example through a revolution. Yet as long as the old system is in place, philosophy cannot become a democratic practice.

To be sure, valuable insights can be gained from such theories. I mentioned above how, after our move to São Paulo, I was surprised by the mother of one of my classmates, who spent hours in front of a crucifix imploring Christ to help her older son get into law school. She thought that her son's success depended on God's will, not his attendance at an expensive private school, followed by an equally pricey preparatory course for the university entrance exam. He was accepted into law school—however only at a second-rate university. That, in turn, didn't affect his job prospects, since God had already arranged for his father to be a senior partner in a law firm in São Paulo. Or consider an example from the other side of the social spectrum: When I worked as a social volunteer for six months in a *favela* in the north of Brazil, I heard inhabitants many times explain their wretched living conditions as divine punishment for sins they had supposedly committed in the past. One needn't be a staunch Marxist to suspect that religion is here being used to justify class privilege and exploitation—as if these somehow expressed the will of God. And there is obviously nothing wrong with using such insights and appealing to these theories in a debate. It is wrong, on the other hand, to turn such a theory into an *authoritative framework* for debating (or, worse, for suppressing debate). Surely these theories (and their spin-offs in contemporary philosophy) are at a minimum fallible and the objects of contestation. In my view they are hardly better grounded than a well reflected religious worldview. There are, moreover, serious religious responses to these theories, some critical, some partly affirmative—for example, the theology of liberation in South America that integrates elements of Marxism into a Christian program for social justice.[84]

My second objection concerns the intellectual elitism I pointed out above. Rather than replacing one system with another under the guidance of intellectuals with supposedly superior knowledge, the culture of debate I propose aims to provide to all citizens tools with which they can change the system on their own if they find fault with it upon careful examination.[85] This culture of debate does not come with a ready-made vision, but expects the vision (or visions) to emerge from the debate. The role of philosophers is not to guide, but to assist in integrating the *practice* of philosophy into our individual and social lives; in this way they can help us to think through questions related to ourselves, our communities, and the world we live in—no matter what answers we ultimately settle on.

Even if the practice of philosophy—that is, the techniques and virtues of debate I mentioned above—becomes part of everyday life through the education system, the degree to which people will, in fact, participate in a culture of debate will surely vary according to inclination, time, and other factors. This adds importance to the reinterpretation of cultural and religious traditions in light of insights gained in the debate—as a means to share the results of the joint search for the truth with everyone, in particular with those who are less engaged in it.

Incorporating considered beliefs and values into cultural and religious traditions through interpretation is also important to bridge the gap between knowing what is right and doing it, or what philosophers call the problem of the weak will. We may know that exercising is good for our health, yet fail to act on it; that biking helps to preserve the environment, yet drive the car; that certain goods were produced under unfair conditions, yet buy them anyway. We do not, in other words, always live by the values we endorse. Plato, Aristotle, and their disciples were keenly aware of this problem. And they proposed a solution: if we are brought up in a culture that embodies what is right, and so are *habituated* to act accordingly from childhood on, then doing what is right will become part of our character. We will, in Aristotle's words, reliably be "attracted by the fine and repulsed by the shameful."[86] As children we will not yet understand the considerations—medical, environmental, moral, and so forth—that shape our character through the culture in which we are brought up. But once we grasp these things, our knowledge of what is right will be in line with what we want.[87] At the same time, ongoing debate allows us to change our mind. The idea of an open-ended culture of debate entails that what is right isn't written in stone once and for all, but remains open to revision from one generation to the next.

ACKNOWLEDGMENTS

This book was in the making for eight years, during which I received a great deal of support. Above all I want to thank the participants in my classes: students from Al-Quds University in East Jerusalem and the State Islamic University in Makassar, members of the Satmar and Lubavitcher Hasidic communities in New York, high school students in Salvador da Bahia (in particular from Colégio Estadual Barros Barreto, Colégio Estadual M. A. Teixeira de Freitas, Colégio Estadual Rotary, Colégio Estadual Thales de Azevedo, and Escola Panamericana), and members of the Mohawk community in Akwesasne. I greatly enjoyed our discussions and came out of them with many new insights and questions.

I wouldn't have been able to organize these classes without the generous help of many people. They include Wendy Adams, Angie Barnes, Phil Buckley, Deborah Corber, Márcio Damin Custódio, Brian David, Wahyuddin Halim, Sarah Herne, Fuad Jabali, Hamdan Juhannis, Ysoscher Katz, Evyatar Marienberg, Sari Nusseibeh, students from the PIBID-Filosofia at the Federal University of Bahia (UFBA), Almira Ribeiro, Sílvia de Assis Saes, Irlan Santos, Gladys Parish Seixas, Genildo da Silva, Gilbert Terrance, and Tadeu Verza.

I am greatly indebted to Michael Walzer who encouraged the project from start to finish and published earlier versions of chapters 1 and 2 in *Dissent.* I am also grateful to Abe Socher who published an earlier version of chapter 3 in the *Jewish Review of Books,* to Deborah Chasman and Josh Cohen who published an earlier version of chapter 4 in *Boston Review,* and to Simon Critchley and Peter Capatano who published excerpts from chapter 6 in the *New York Times.* My writing has benefited from their editorial and intellectual input.

It's been delightful to discuss my ideas with Adam Etinson, formerly a student, now a colleague and friend. In particular two political philosophy classes we cotaught at McGill helped me to clarify the project's theoretical framework. Adam and I also collaborated on setting up and teaching the classes in Akwesasne. Probing discussions with Stephen Menn left their mark on every page of the book. Steven Nadler offered helpful comments at various stages of the project. Other colleagues who gave me valuable feedback include Ricardo Andrade, Julie Cooper, Tom Laqueur, Charles Taylor, Michael Weinman, and Rafael Ziegler. I also gratefully acknowledge a fellowship from the German Humboldt-Foundation that enabled me to spend a year in Berlin working on the book. During that year, I greatly enjoyed the conversations with my sponsor, Dominik Perler.

Rob Tempio and the staff from Princeton University Press handled the book with care and efficiency; it was a pleasure to collaborate with them. Two anonymous reviewers for the press contributed perceptive comments that helped me with the final revision. Marguerite Pigeon superbly edited the manuscript for style and content, Zoli Filotas prepared an excellent index, and Eva Andermann meticulously proofread the book.

Finally, I would like to thank my wife, Anne, a first-class debater, for reading earlier versions of most of the chapters and for putting my ideas to the test. "What's wrong? I thought you like a culture of debate!" she often reminds me when we don't see eye to eye on something. I dedicate this book to my children, Lara and Ben (my first book I hope they'll actually read), and to the memory of my grandfather, Joaquim Câmara Ferreira, whom I never met, but whose life and commitment I admire. The book owes much to all three of them.

NOTES

PREFACE

1. See the *Ilahiyāt* of Avicenna's *Kitāb al-shifāʿ*, bk. 1, chap. 6.

CHAPTER 1. TEACHING PLATO IN PALESTINE

1. On the translation movement, see Gutas (1998).
2. Oz (2005, 3).
3. On the concept of a philosophical religion, see Fraenkel (2012), especially chap. 3 on al-Fārābī, Averroes, and Maimonides.
4. *Letters*, 553.
5. *Eight Chapters*, Arabic 373; Eng. 60.
6. See Cowell (2005).
7. See Nusseibeh (2007, chap. 21).
8. See Nusseibeh (2007, 260–61).
9. Nusseibeh (2001).
10. Nusseibeh and Ayalon (2002).
11. Note that Nusseibeh's position on a two-state solution seems to have shifted more recently; see Nusseibeh (2012).
12. See *Apology* 38a.
13. See ibid., 40c–41c.
14. Herodotus, *Histories* 3.38.
15. Note that this chapter was written several years before the so-called Arab spring. The change in the political landscape supports the case for philosophy, since citizens in many parts of the Middle East now have more possibilities to put their political ideas into practice.
16. See Stroumsa (1999, chap. 3).
17. See *Refutation of the Logicians*, esp. secs. 319–21.
18. On Islamic political thought, see, for example, Crone (2004).
19. See *Republic* 6, 488a–489a.
20. See *Republic* 2, 359a–360d.
21. On al-Fārābī's concept of religion, see Fraenkel (2012, chap. 3).
22. See, for example, al-Fārābī, *The Attainment of Happiness*, Arabic 185; Eng. 45, and Maimonides, *Guide of the Perplexed* 1.8–9.
23. See again Fraenkel (2012, chap. 3).

24. For the recognition of Buddhism as a valid religion by Indonesian Muslims, see chapter 2.

25. For more on this issue, see the section "An Ethnocentric Project?" in chapter 6.

CHAPTER 2. TEACHING MAIMONIDES IN MAKASSAR

1. See *Republic* 5, 473c–e. In addition to knowing the good, one must also have the moral integrity to act on this knowledge, which Plato attributes to philosophers as well. See bk. 7, 520d–521a.

2. Note that Plato's intellectual elitism rules this out. I briefly address this issue in chapters 4 and 6.

3. *Theaetetus* 174a.

4. See chapter 1.

5. But see chapter 4 on Brazil, where philosophy is, in fact, part of the high school curriculum and considered a condition for good citizenship.

6. See Martin and Woodward (1998, pt. 2), especially chaps. 8 and 9.

7. The definitive account of early Muslim theology is van Ess (1991–97).

8. *Book of the Five Principles*, Arabic 79; Eng. 90.

9. See the account of the debates between the schools of Basra and Baghdad in Abū Rashīd al-Nisābūrī. For a debate with members of other religions, see the text by al-Humaydī quoted in chapter 6.

10. On Muʿtazilite politics, see Crone (2004, chap. 6).

11. But note Amartya Sen (2005), who argues that the long tradition of vigorous intellectual debate in India was an important factor for the success of democracy there.

12. See Said (1978) and the broad discussion that followed.

13. See the case for cultural contamination in Appiah (2006, chap. 7). In my view, Appiah doesn't pay sufficient attention to the importance of equipping people with the tools to make good decisions.

14. See *Nicomachean Ethics* 10.6–8.

15. This, at least, is, in a nutshell, my interpretation of Aristotle's ethics.

16. See *Nicomachean Ethics* 10.9.

17. See the end of his work on Islamic jurisprudence: *Bidāyat al-mujtahid* 57.6.

18. See Sakai and Fauzia (2014). While they conclude that "Is-

lamism" is on the rise, they argue that it is not political, but cultural Islamism: the desire to live by Muslim values rather than the desire to impose them through political power.

19. Hefner (2000, 14).

20. See, for example, Farish A. Noor's 2006 interview with Bashir.

21. For a good account of modern Indonesian history, see Vickers (2005).

22. See the evidence quoted in Hefner (2005) showing that 60 percent of Indonesian Muslims voted for non-Islamist parties in the 1999 elections.

23. Geertz (1960, 40).

24. As already briefly discussed in chapter 1. For al-Fārābī's concept of religion, see again Fraenkel (2012, chap. 3).

25. Madjid (1994, 71).

26. On Islam and *Pancasila*, see Ismail (2001).

27. Though Lessing's *Nathan the Wise*, an important document of the German Enlightenment, proposes a similar idea.

CHAPTER 3. SPINOZA IN SHTREIMELS: AN UNDERGROUND SEMINAR

1. Here and throughout, I have changed names and some details to preserve the anonymity of my students.

2. The historical Marranos were Jews on the Iberian Peninsula who were forced to convert to Christianity after the 1492 Spanish Edict of Expulsion, but often held on to Judaism in secret. In a sense, my students were inverted Marranos.

3. *Shul* is the Yiddish word for synagogue, *Shabbos* the Ashkenazi pronunciation of Shabbat.

4. At least this is the concept of God that Plato attributes to Socrates in the *Phaedo*; see 97c.

5. *Republic* 9, 588c–d.

6. See Epicurus's *Letter to Menoeceus* for a summary of his ethical doctrines.

7. See *Deliverance from Error*, Arabic 100; Eng. 38–39.

8. Compare Fenton (1997).

9. See Kant's *Groundwork of the Metaphysics of Morals.*

10. For the discussion of al-Ghazālī here and below, see *Deliverance from Error*, Arabic 65–77; Eng. 19–26.

11. See *Be'ur ha-Gra on Shulhan ʿarukh*, Yoreh Deʿah 179:6.

12. See Zeitlin (1900).

13. See *Theological-Political Treatise* 1 and 4 for Spinoza's portrait of Christ as a philosopher.

14. Hillel and Shammai were two leading rabbinic scholars of the first century BCE. The debates between them and their schools—*Bet Hillel* and *Bet Shammai*—are recorded in the Talmud. For the saying quoted by Abraham, see *Babylonian Talmud*, Treatise Eruvin, 13b.

15. See, for example, *The Gay Science*, sec. 125.

16. Nietzsche's critique of religion—in particular, of Christianity—runs through his writings. For a particularly sharp statement, see his late work, *The Anti-Christ.*

17. See Maimonides, *Book of Knowledge*, Laws Concerning Repentance 10.5; Spinoza, *Ethics* 5, propositions 41 and 42.

18. See, for example, *The Gay Science*, sec. 290.

19. See the notion of the "sovereign individual" in *On the Genealogy of Morals* 2, sec. 2 and the instructions for attaining self-control in *Daybreak* 2, sec. 109.

20. See the references given in note 19.

21. See *Republic* 2, 369b and *Ethics* 4, proposition 35, note to corollary 2.

22. See *Guide of the Perplexed* 3.54.

23. Sec. 341.

CHAPTER 4. CITIZEN PHILOSOPHERS IN BRAZIL

1. Just to be clear: I am not claiming that they are involved in drugs because they are black, but because of socioeconomic conditions that for historical reasons often correlate with race in Brazil.

2. See law no. 11.684 that modifies article 36 of law 9.394.

3. See *Republic* 7, 538c–539a.

4. See *Republic* 6, 473c–e.

5. I return to this question at the end of chapter 6.

6. The standard account of the institutional history of philosophy in Brazil is Arantes (1994).

7. The movement's best known representative is the Argentinean philosopher Enrique Dussel; see, for example, Dussel (1980).

8. For the relationships between husband, wife, and slaves in a household, see *Politics* 1, 1254b13–14. For Plato's brand of gender egalitarianism, see *Republic* 5, 456a.

9. See Maxwell (1975, chaps. 5 and 6).

10. In fairness to Brazilian academic philosophers, it is worth asking whether academic philosophers elsewhere are more engaged with

local concerns and would have shown greater enthusiasm if philosophy had become an obligatory high school subject in their countries.

11. *Symposium* 210a–212c.

CHAPTER 5. WORD-WARRIORS: PHILOSOPHY IN MOHAWK LAND

1. For the traditional view, see the account of Akwesasne historian Darren Bonaparte (2006).
2. For background, see Tobias (1991).
3. Davenport (1967, Latin 16; Eng. 23).
4. The most important statement of De las Casas's view is *In Defense of the Indians.*
5. For background, see Tarbell and Arquette (2000).
6. Compare my account in chapter 3 of how al-Ghazālī loses faith in Islam as he imagines himself growing up as a Jew or Christian; see also chapter 6.
7. See Pasquaretta (1994, 703–7).
8. See Turner (2006).
9. On the ethical questions raised by the collapse of an Indigenous culture, see Lear (2006).
10. Smith (1870, 144–45).
11. See *Republic* 2, 359a–360d.
12. On the Oka crisis, see York and Pindera (1991).
13. See again Tobias (1991).
14. On the White Paper and its reception in Indigenous communities, see Turner (2006, chap. 1).
15. *The Jesuit Relations*, 57–58.
16. Alfred (1999, 25).
17. Lafitau (1974, 69).
18. Parker (1916, 30).
19. See Plato's discussion in *Republic* 5 and Aristotle's response in *Politics* 2.5.
20. *Reasons and Considerations Touching the Lawfulness of Removing Out of England into the Parts of America*, 242.
21. Mill, *On Liberty*, 14.

CHAPTER 6. DIVERSITY AND DEBATE

1. For my childhood impersonation of Winnetou, see chapter 5.
2. This idealized picture of Germany, I should note, foundered soon enough—when my grandmother (who had escaped Germany in

1939 on a *Kindertransport* to England) ran out of patience and gave me a copy of *Der Gelbe Stern*, a photo documentary of the Holocaust, billed as "the world's most shocking *Bilderbuch*."

3. See Fukuyama (1992).

4. Taylor (1989, chap. 1).

5. For other accounts of how disruption can spark philosophical inquiry, see the examples in part 1 of the book: experiencing the Israeli-Palestinian conflict from opposite perspectives (chapter 1); being a member of a—from the standpoint of the mainstream—"strange" minority like Hasidic Judaism (chapter 3); and growing up with the tensions in a mixed-race family in Brazil (chapter 4). In Brazil and Cairo I found out for myself what it means to belong to a "strange" minority.

6. See Plato on the quest for the true good (for example, *Apology* 38a), Aristotle on the connection between knowledge and happiness (for example, *Nicomachean Ethics* 10.8, 1178b28–31), and Kant on the moral obligation to tell the truth (for example, *On the Supposed Right to Lie from Philanthropy*). For God as *al-Ḥaqq* in the Quran, see sūra 22:6. But note that it is by no means *obvious* that discovering the truth is a good thing. Consider the pessimistic views of the human condition proposed from Schopenhauer onward. Albert Camus, for example, argues in the *Myth of Sisyphus* that while we can't avoid searching for meaning, we are condemned to fail in a meaningless world. Yet, like Sisyphus, we go at it again and again—a life of "futility and hopeless labor" (119). So the key question for Camus is whether we should commit suicide, once we realize the absurdity of our situation. Compare the nausea that befalls Antoine Roquentin in Sartre's *Nausea* after he realizes the meaninglessness of his life. Are we, then, better off discovering the truth or living in the comfort of false hope and illusion?

7. *Philosophical Commentary* 1.5, French 120; Eng. 52.

8. Ibid.

9. Ibid., French 120; Eng. 51.

10. See chapter 5.

11. *Dissoi Logoi* 2.9–15.

12. Ibid., 2.18.

13. The diversity of beliefs and values is also often used as evidence for relativism. Note that fallibilism and relativism need not be mutually exclusive. Some things may indeed just be conventions, tastes, or fashions—eating etiquettes, for example, preferring Beethoven over Bach, or bell-bottom over straight-leg jeans, and so forth. In these cases there likely is no objective right or wrong.

14. Compare the experience described by Jacob, one of my Hasidic students, in chapter 3. For a contemporary version of this "argument from symmetry," see Kitcher (2011, 26): "Most Christians have adopted their doctrines much as the polytheists and the ancestor-worshippers have acquired theirs, through early teaching and socialization. Had the Christians been born among the aboriginal Australians, they would believe, in just the same ways, on just the same bases, and with just the same convictions, doctrines about the Dreamtime instead of about the Resurrection. The symmetry is complete."

15. *Apology* 30e.

16. Ibid., 31a.

17. *On the Order of His Own Books* 1.19, 50. On the historical connection between Galen and al-Ghazālī, see Menn (2003).

18. See *Against Celsus* 1.10 and the description of Origen's curriculum in Gregory Thaumaturgus's *Address of Thanksgiving to Origen* 13–14.

19. This is a key insight in social psychology going back to the experiments that Solomon Asch conducted in the 1950s. Recently, Jonathan Haidt has argued for the "importance of social and cultural influences" on our value judgments. See Haidt (2001). I hope to explore the implications of my project for the findings of social psychologists in the future. For an earlier account of the problem, see Mill's concept of the "tyranny of the majority" that I discuss below.

20. It would, of course, be impossible (as well as silly) to subject *all* our beliefs to critical examination. In day-to-day life it often makes sense to submit to *taqlīd*: I trust that money will come out of the ATM machine, that the fridge will keep my milk refrigerated, and so forth.

21. *On the History of Scholars in al-Andalus*, 175–76.

22. Note that I don't mean to say that the theory of evolution is controversial *among scientists* or that I consider it controversial.

23. *Republic* 9, 581a.

24. Of course higher education, too, can make an important contribution to such a culture. See, for example, Martha Nussbaum (1997), who defends reform in liberal education that aims to replace the canon of dead, white, male authors with one reflecting society's true diversity—sexual, cultural, racial, and so forth. Exposing students to such diversity, Nussbaum argues, needn't lead to complacent relativism, but is an opportunity for Socratic examination. My reason for proposing to anchor a culture of debate in high school is that it allows *all* citizens to participate in it.

25. *Letter 93*, 58.

26. For a recent fallibilist argument for toleration, see Popper

(1987). Note that I am not claiming that fallibilism is the only or even the best argument for tolerating disagreement. Following Kant we could argue that we ought to respect the autonomy of all human beings even if we think that they are wrong. Or, following John Stuart Mill, we could argue that we must respect their individuality since, on utilitarian grounds, it is more important to be true to oneself than to be right. I do think, however, that the fallibilist argument is *more widely* acceptable than alternative arguments. Most of the participants in my workshops rank living a pious life according to God's will higher than living autonomously or expressing their individuality. We can discuss the value of autonomy and individuality with them, but we cannot appeal to these values to establish the conditions for the discussion. For a more detailed account of Kant and Mill, see the next section. Of course someone can be tolerant for reasons other than fallibility or for multiple reasons (for example, fallibility and respect for autonomy). Note, however, that not *all* reasons for toleration are good reasons, as I will argue below.

27. See *Book of Knowledge*, Commandments Concerning the Foundations of the Law.

28. *Republic* 6, 511b.

29. *Principles of Philosophy*, preface to the French translation.

30. Note that the argument from *diaphônia* (disagreement) was originally used to support skepticism (see Sextus Empiricus, *Outlines of Pyrrhonism* 1.65). It can, however, be used in support of fallibilism as well. Of course much more needs to be said to defend fallibilism against infallibilists, but here is not the place for a detailed discussion. Below I address challenges from the opposite side of the epistemological spectrum—those of skeptics and relativists.

31. See Menachem Fisch (1997) who makes a convincing case for such a program in the Babylonian Talmud.

32. Gregory Thaumaturgus, *Address of Thanksgiving to Origen* 13.153.

33. At the end of his discussion of Christ's incarnation, for example, Origen writes that "if someone could find something better" than the solution he proposed, "then his words rather than ours should be accepted" (*On First Principles* 2.6, 7).

34. Note, however, that al-Ghazālī does not actually report having examined other religious traditions. After the skeptical crisis, triggered by the breaking of *taqlīd*, he turns directly to examining the different interpretations of Islam.

35. *The Decisive Criterion for Distinguishing Islam from Unbelief*, Arabic 175–89; Eng. 96–103.

36. See Averroes's argument in the *Decisive Treatise* and Maimonides's argument in the *Guide of the Perplexed.*

37. See, in particular, Robert Wisnovsky's forthcoming book on postclassical Arabic philosophy from 1100 to 1900.

38. *Confessions* 7.9, 13.

39. *Against the Academicians* 3.20.

40. *Philosophical Commentary* 1.5, French 120; Eng. 52.

41. *Eight Chapters*, Arabic 373; Eng. 60.

42. *Letters*, 553; see also chapter 1.

43. Shlomo Pines, the great historian of Islamic and Jewish thought, went so far as to say that "in its decisive period mediaeval Jewish thought was an offshoot of Arabic thought: the debates of Jewish philosophers can only be understood" against the background of "the doctrinal differences obtaining among Arabic philosophers" (Pines 1959). There is, however, no need to describe medieval Jewish philosophy pejoratively as an "offshoot." Jewish philosophers in the Islamic world are simply participating in the intellectual culture of their time. They frequently stand out through the originality of their responses to its central philosophical, theological, and scientific concerns—regardless of the fact that they were Jews who wrestled with these questions in a Jewish context.

44. See chapter 3 for a more detailed discussion.

45. My aim is not to draw a simplistic dichotomy between an "enlightened" medieval approach to religion and a "bigotted" modern approach. There are, of course, many modern examples of the practice of reinterpreting religious traditions, as well as medieval examples of the rejection of this practice. The medieval thinkers, however, illustrate my point particularly well and show that this practice has a long and distinguished history. For an extensive discussion of the philosophical reinterpretation of religious traditions, see Fraenkel (2012).

46. See Averroes, *Long Commentary on the* Metaphysics, Arabic 1634; Eng. 166, and *Decisive Treatise*, Arabic and Eng. 2; Maimonides, *Book of Knowledge*, Laws Concerning Idolatry 1.3 and *Guide of the Perplexed* 3.29, Arabic 376; Eng. 514–15.

47. There is, however, an important objection to this approach. Many of us feel that there is something wrong with the portrait of Abraham as an accomplished Aristotelian philosopher. And part of why we feel that way is because we were trained to read the Bible according to the historical-critical method. One of the pioneers of the historical-critical method was Spinoza in the *Theological-Political Treatise* (see esp. chap. 7). Spinoza targets Maimonides directly: if we read the Bible on its own terms, he argues, we find no evidence for

the claim that Abraham—or any of the patriarchs and prophets for that matter—was a great philosopher. According to Spinoza we cannot simply interpret the Bible in light of the beliefs we hold true. Instead we must determine the Bible's true meaning through a rigorous philological and historical-contextual method. Only after establishing its true meaning can we ask whether it is true. Then we will find out, Spinoza argues, that most of the Bible's teachings—especially on theoretical matters, such as God and nature—are false. The commitment to the truth thus risks undermining itself: first it will lead religious believers to interpret their religious tradition in light of the beliefs they hold true. Then it will lead them to reject that interpretation in the name of the historical truth. I have not yet found a solution to this problem.

48. *Meno* 97e–98a.

49. Spinoza's argument for freedom of thought and expression in the *Theological-Political Treatise*, for example, does not presuppose a liberal-democratic framework, nor does Kant's in *An Answer to the Question: What is Enlightenment?*

50. See his *Refutation of the Logicians*, esp. secs. 319–21. For background and context, see Hallaq's introduction to the English translation. The *Refutation* consists, of course, in a sophisticated *argument* against the validity of central categories of Aristotelian logic, illustrating Aristotle's claim in the *Protrepticus* that even the opponents of philosophy need to rely on philosophy to explain why they reject it.

51. Likewise, skeptics and relativists may value the truth, but deny that it is possible to find it. Hence they, too, would have no interest in a culture of debate. I discuss skepticism and relativism below.

52. See *Groundwork of the Metaphysics of Morals*, German 393; Eng. 49.

53. *An Answer to the Question: What is Enlightenment?*, German 36; Eng. 18.

54. *On the Supposed Right to Lie from Philanthropy*.

55. *An Answer to the Question: What is Enlightenment?*, German 35; Eng. 17.

56. Ibid., German 36; Eng. 18.

57. See *On Liberty*, pt. 3.

58. Ibid., 9.

59. Ibid., 23.

60. Ibid., 8–9.

61. Ibid., 9.

62. Ibid., 40.

63. Ibid., 41.
64. Ibid., 40.
65. Ibid., 50.
66. See *A Theory of Justice*, chap. 3, in particular sec. 24.
67. Ibid., chap. 2.
68. Ibid., chap. 3, sec. 24. Rawls explicitly includes the "laws of human psychology" among the "general facts" known behind the veil of ignorance (119).
69. See Peter Jones (2006) for a critical discussion of the shift in the discourse on toleration—from tolerating beliefs and values that we disagree with to celebrating and affirming diversity. See also Rainer Forst's helpful conceptual map in Forst (2013).
70. Sec. 3.1 (h), 4.
71. Bernard Williams called this argument "the anthropologist's fallacy" and described it as "possibly the most absurd view to have been advanced even in moral philosophy." See Williams (1972, 20). For an attempt to defend a relativist case for toleration, see Wong (1984, chap. 12).
72. See the critique of relativism in Taylor (1992). Note that Taylor, too, endorses a "politics of recognition"—not, however, on relativist grounds. He claims that we ought to "presume" that other cultures have value. This presumption will then be confirmed or disproved through subsequent examination. See Taylor (1994, 66–68).
73. For the popularity of relativism, see Bloom (1987).
74. For a defense of relativism, see, for example, Wong (1984).
75. See, for example, Nussbaum (1993).
76. See Raz (1986, 395). For an influential statement of value pluralism, see Berlin (1988).
77. For a classic statement of this charge, see Said (1978).
78. See Adorno (1951). Note, however, that they have not disappeared; they inform, for example, much of contemporary Western anti-Muslim polemics.
79. *Republic* 5, 473c–e.
80. As we will see shortly, the attempt to enlighten nonphilosophers fails according to the *Republic* (see bk. 7, 517a). Here I only want to distance myself from the authority that Plato attributes to the philosopher's knowledge.
81. See *Republic* 7, 538c–539a.
82. Marx, Nietzsche, and Freud were the three master practitioners of what Paul Ricoeur aptly called "the hermeneutics of suspicion." See Ricoeur (1965, bk. 1.2).

83. See, for example, Herbert Marcuse (1969).

84. See Gutiérrez (1971).

85. Note that the step from finding fault with the system to changing it presupposes a political order in which citizens have political power. As I said above, a culture of debate doesn't depend on such a political order.

86. *Nicomachean Ethics* 10.9, 1179b31–36.

87. Unlike Plato and Aristotle, however, who think that the state should enforce values, I propose making them part of existing religious and cultural traditions through interpretation.

BIBLIOGRAPHY

Abd al-Jabbār, *Book of the Five Principles* [*Kitāb al-uṣūl al-khamsa*], Arabic in D. Gimaret, "Les *Uṣūl al-ḫamsa* du Qāḍī 'Abd al-Ǧabbār et leurs commentaires," *Annales Islamologiques* 15 (1979), 47–96; Eng. trans. in Martin and Woodward, *Defenders of Reason in Islam.*

Abū Rashīd al-Nīsābūrī, *Book of Questions Concerning Which There Is Disagreement between the Schools of Basra and Baghdad* [*Kitāb al-masā'il fī al-khilāf bayna al-Baṣarīyīn wa-al-Baghdādīyīn*], taḥqīq wa-taqdīm Maʿan Ziyāda, Raḍwān al-Sayyid, Ṭarābulus, al-Jamāhīrīya al-ʿArabīya al-Lībīya al-Shaʿbīya al-Ishtirāqīya: Maʿhad al-Inmā' al-ʿArabī, 1979.

Adorno, Theodor W., *Minima Moralia: Reflections from Damaged Life* [*Minima Moralia: Reflexionen aus dem beschädigten Leben*], Frankfurt: Suhrkamp, 1951; Eng. trans. E. Jephcott, London: New Left Books, 1974.

Al-Fārābī, *The Attainment of Happiness* [*Taḥṣīl al-saʿāda*], in *al-Aʿmāl al-falsafiyya*, ed. J. Al-Yasin, 119–225, Beirut, 1992; Eng. trans. M. Mahdi in *Al-Farabi's Philosophy of Plato and Aristotle*, Ithaca, NY: Cornell University Press, 1962.

Alfred, Taiaiake, *Peace, Power, Righteousness: An Indigenous Manifesto*, Oxford: Oxford University Press, 1999.

Al-Ghazālī, *The Decisive Criterion for Distinguishing Islam from Unbelief* [*Fayṣal al-tafriqa bayna al-Islām wa-al-zandaqa*], ed. S. Dunyā, Cairo: ʿĪsā al-Bābī al-Ḥalabī, 1961; Eng. trans. S. A. Jackson in *On the Boundaries of Theological Tolerance in Islam: Abū Ḥāmid al-Ghazālī's Fayṣal al-Tafriqa*, Oxford: Oxford University Press, 2002.

——, *The Deliverance from Error* [*Munqidh min al-ḍalāl*], ed. J. Saliba and K. Ayyad, Damascus, 1939; Eng. trans. W. M. Watt in *The Faith and Practice of Al-Ghazālī*, London: George Allen and Unwin, 1953.

Al-Humaydī, *On the History of Scholars in al-Andalus* [*Jadhwat al-muqtabis fī ta'rīkh 'ulamā' al-Andalus*], ed. Ibrāhīm al-Ibyārī, Beirut: Dār al-Kitāb al-Lubnānī, 1983.

Appiah, Kwame A., *Cosmopolitanism: Ethics in a World of Strangers*, New York: Norton, 2006.

Arantes, Paulo, *Um departamento francês de ultramar: Estudos sobre a formação da cultura filosófica uspiana*, São Paulo: Paz e Terra, 1994.

Aristotle, *Nicomachean Ethics*, Greek in I. Bywater, *Aristotelis ethica Nicomachea*, Oxford: Clarendon, 1894; Eng. trans. S. Broadie and C. Rowe, Oxford: Oxford University Press, 2002.

——, *Politics*, in W.D. Ross, *Aristotelis politica*, Oxford: Clarendon, 1957; Eng. trans. in *The Complete Works of Aristotle*, ed. J. Barnes, Princeton: Princeton University Press, 1984.

——, *Protrepticus*, Greek in I. Düring, *Aristotle's Protrepticus*, Stockholm: Almqvist and Wiksell, 1961; Eng. trans. in *The Complete Works of Aristotle*, ed. J. Barnes, Princeton: Princeton University Press, 1984.

Augustine, *Against the Academicians* [*Contra Academicos*], Latin in *CSEL* 63 (1922); Eng. trans. P. King in *Against the Academicians and the Teacher*, Indianapolis: Hackett, 1995.

——, *Complete Works*, in *Corpus Scriptorum Ecclesiasticorum Latinorum*, Vienna: Tempsky, 1865–(=*CSEL*).

——, *Confessions*, Latin in *CSEL* 33 (1869); Eng. trans. H. Chadwick, Oxford: Oxford University Press, 1991.

——, *Letter 93*, Latin in *CSEL* 34.2 (1898); Eng. trans. W. Parsons in *Saint Augustine, Letters*, vol. 2, Washington, DC: Catholic University of America Press, 1953.

Austin, John L., *How to Do Things with Words*, ed. M. Sbisà and J. O. Urmson, Oxford: Oxford University Press, 1962.

Averroes, *Bidāyat al-mujtahid wa-nihāyat al-muqtaṣid*, 2 vols., Cairo: al-Maktaba al-Tijāriyya al-Kubrā, 1952. Eng. trans. Imran Ahsan Khan Nyazee in *The Distinguished Jurist's Primer*, 2 vols., Reading: Centre for Muslim Contribution to Civilization, 1994–96.

——, *Decisive Treatise* [*Faṣl al-maqāl*], Arabic G. Hourani (corrections by M. Mahdi), Eng. trans. C. Butterworth, Provo: Brigham Young University Press, 2001.

——, *Long Commentary on the* Metaphysics [*Tafsīr mā baʿd al-ṭabīʿāt*], ed. M. Bouyges, Imprimerie Catholique, Beirut 1938–48; Eng. trans. of *Metaphysics* 12 in C. Genequand, *Ibn Rushd's Metaphysics*, Brill: Leiden, 1984.

Avicenna, *The Metaphysics of the Healing* [*Kitāb al-shifāʿ: al-Ilahiyāt*], ed. and Eng. trans. M. Marmura, Provo: Brigham Young University Press, 2005.

Bayle, Pierre, *Philosophical Commentary on These Words of Jesus Christ, Compel Them to Come In* [*Commentaire philosophique sur ces paroles de Jésus-Christ, Contrains-les d'entrer*], ed. J.-M. Gros, Paris: Honoré Champion, 2006; Eng. trans. A. Tannenbaum in *Pierre Bayle's* Philosophical Commentary*: A Modern Translation and Critical Interpretation*, Bern: Peter Lang, 1987.

Berlin, Isaiah, "On the Pursuit of the Ideal," *New York Review of Books*, 17 March 1988, 11–18.

Bloom, Allan, *The Closing of the American Mind*, New York: Simon & Schuster, 1987.

Bonaparte, Darren, *Creation and Confederation: The Living History of the Iroquois*, Akwesasne: Wampum Chronicles, 2006.

Camus, Albert, *Le Mythe de Sisyphe*, Paris: Gallimard, 1943; Eng. trans. J. O'Brien in *The Myth of Sisyphus and Other Essays*, New York: Knopf, 1955.

Cowell, Allan, "End to Boycott of Israeli Universities Is Urged," *New York Times*, 20 May 2005.

Crone, Patricia, *God's Rule: Government and Islam: Six Centuries of Islamic Political Thought*, New York: Columbia University Press, 2004.

Cushman, Robert, *Reasons and Considerations Touching the Lawfulness of Removing Out of England into the Parts of America*, in A. Young, *Chronicles of the Pilgrim Fathers of the Colony of Plymouth*, Boston: Little, Brown, 1841, 242–46.

Davenport, Frances, *European Treaties Bearing on the History of the United States and Its Dependencies to 1648*, Washington, DC: Carnegie Institution of Washington, 1967.

De las Casas, Bartolomé, *In Defense of the Indians*, Eng. trans. Stafford Poole, DeKalb: Northern Illinois University Press, 1992.

Descartes, René, *Principles of Philosophy* [*Principia Philosophiae*] in *Oeuvres de Descartes*, vol. 8, ed. C. Adam and P. Tannery, Paris: CNRS/Vrin, 1964–74; Eng. trans. J. Cottingham, R. Stoothoff, D. Murdoch, and A. Kenny in *The Philosophical Writings of Descartes*, vol. 1, Cambridge: Cambridge University Press, 1984–91.

Dissoi Logoi, in T. M. Robinson, *Contrasting Arguments: An Edition of the* Dissoi Logoi, New York: Arno Series, 1979.

Dussel, Enrique, *Filosofía de la liberación*, Bogotá: Universidad Santo Tomás, 1980; Eng. trans. A. Martinez and C. Morkovsky, Maryknoll, NY: Orbis Books, 1985.

Elijah ben Solomon Zalman (Vilna Gaon), *Commentary on the Shulhan ʿarukh* [*Beʾur ha-Gra on Shulhan ʿarukh*], appended to most editions of the *Shulhan ʿaruk*.

Epicurus, *Letter to Menoeceus*, in A. A. Long and D. Sedley, *The Hellenistic Philosophers*, Cambridge: Cambridge University Press, 1987.

Ess, Josef van, *Theologie und Gesellschaft im 2. und 3. Jahrhundert Hidschra: Eine Geschichte des religiösen Denkens im frühen Islam*, Berlin: Walter de Gruyter, 1991–97.

Fenton, Paul, "Judaeo-Arabic Mystical Writings of the XIIIth–XIVth

Centuries," in *Judaeo-Arabic Studies*, ed. N. Golb, London: Routledge, 1997, 87–101.

Fisch, Menachem, *Rational Rabbis: Science and Talmudic Culture*, Bloomington: Indiana University Press, 1997.

Forst, Rainer, *Toleration in Conflict: Past and Present*, Eng. trans. C. Croni, Cambridge: Cambridge University Press, 2013.

Fraenkel, Carlos, *Philosophical Religions from Plato to Spinoza: Reason, Religion, and Autonomy*, Cambridge: Cambridge University Press, 2012.

Frankfurt, Harry, *On Bullshit*, Princeton: Princeton University Press, 2005.

Fukuyama, Francis, *The End of History and the Last Man*, New York: Free Press, 1992.

Galen, *On the Order of His Own Books* [*De ordine librorum suorum*], in Galen, *Opera omnia*, ed. C. G. Kühn, Leipzig: Knoblauch, 1821–33.

Geertz, Clifford, *The Religion of Java*, Chicago: University of Chicago Press, 1960.

Greer, Allan, ed., *The Jesuit Relations: Natives and Missionaries in Seventeenth-Century North America*, Boston: Bedford/St. Martin's, 2000.

Gregory Thaumaturgus, *Address of Thanksgiving to Origen* [*In Originem oratio panegyrica*], Greek with French trans. H. Crouzel in Grégoire Le Thaumaturge, *Remerciement à Origène—suivi de la lettre d'Origène à Grégoire*, Paris: Edition du Cerf, 1969; Eng. trans. M. Slusser in *St. Gregory Thaumaturgus: Life and Works*, Washington, DC: Catholic University of America Press, 1998.

Gutas, Dimitri, *Greek Thought, Arabic Culture: The Graeco-Arabic Translation Movement in Baghdad and Early Abbasid Society*, London: Routledge, 1998.

Gutiérrez, Gustavo, *Teología de la liberación: Perspectivas*, Lima: Centro de Estudios y Publicaciones, 1971; Eng. trans. C. Inda and J. Eagleson in *A Theology of Liberation: History, Politics, and Salvation*, Maryknoll, NY: Orbis, 1973.

Haidt, Jonathan, "The Emotional Dog and Its Rational Tail: A Social Intuitionist Approach to Moral Judgment," *Psychological Review* 108 (2001), 814–34.

Hefner, Robert, *Civil Islam: Muslims and Democratization in Indonesia*, Princeton: Princeton University Press, 2000.

——, "Muslim Democrats and Islamist Violence in Post-Soeharto Indonesia," in *Remaking Muslim Politics*, ed. R. Hefner, Princeton: Princeton University Press, 2005, 273–301.

Herodotus, *Histories*, in H. B. Rosén, *Herodoti* Historiae, Leipzig: Teubner, 1987; Eng. trans. D. Grene, Chicago: University of Chicago Press, 1988.

Ibn Taymiyya, *Refutation of the Logicians* [*al-Radd ʿala al-manṭiqiyyin*], Eng. trans. W. Hallaq in *Against the Greek Logicians*, Oxford: Oxford University Press, 1993.

Ismail, Faisal, *Islam and Pancasila*, Jakarta: Departemen Agama, 2001.

Jones, Peter, "Toleration, Recognition and Identity," *Journal of Political Philosophy* 14 (2006), 123–43.

Kant, Immanuel, *An Answer to the Question: What Is Enlightenment?* [*Beantwortung der Frage: Was ist Aufklärung?*], in *Kants gesammelte Schriften*, Akademie-Ausgabe, vol. 8, Berlin: Walter De Gruyter, 1900–; Eng. trans. M. J. Gregor in Immanuel Kant, *Practical Philosophy*, Cambridge: Cambridge University Press, 1996.

——, *Groundwork of the Metaphysics of Morals*, Akademie-Ausgabe, vol. 4; Eng. trans. M. J. Gregor in Immanuel Kant, *Practical Philosophy*, Cambridge: Cambridge University Press, 1996.

——, *On the Supposed Right to Lie from Philanthropy*, Akademie-Ausgabe, vol. 8; Eng. trans. M. J. Gregor in Immanuel Kant, *Practical Philosophy*, Cambridge: Cambridge University Press, 1996.

Kitcher, Philip, "Challenges for Secularism," in *The Joy of Secularism*, ed. George Levine, Princeton: Princeton University Press, 2011, 24–56.

Lafitau, Joseph-François, *Customs of the American Indians Compared with the Customs of Primitive Times*, 2 vols., Eng. trans. and ed. William Fenton and Elizabeth Moore, Toronto: Champlain Society, 1974 and 1977.

Lear, Jonathan, *Radical Hope: Ethics in the Face of Cultural Devastation*, Cambridge, MA: Harvard University Press, 2006.

Lessing, Gotthold Ephraim, *Nathan the Wise* [*Nathan der Weise*], in *Werke und Briefe in zwölf Bänden*, vol. 9, ed. Wilfried Barner et al., Frankfurt: Deutscher Klassiker Verlag, 1989–94; Eng. trans. P. Maxwell, New York: Bloch, 1939.

Madjid, Nurcholish, "Islamic Roots of Modern Pluralism: Indonesian Experiences," *Studia Islamika* 1 (1994), 55–77.

Maimonides, *Book of Knowledge* [*Sefer ha-maddaʿ*], Jerusalem: Mosad ha-Rav Kook, 1993; Eng. trans. M. Hyamson, New York: Feldheim, 1981.

——, *Eight Chapters*, Arabic in *Mishnah im perush rabbenu Mosheh ben Maimon*, ed. J. Kafih, Jerusalem: Mosad ha-Rav Kook, 1963–68; Eng. trans. C. Butterworth and R. Weiss in *Ethical Writings of Maimonides*, New York: Dover, 1975.

——, *Guide of the Perplexed* [*Dalālat al-ḥāʾirīn*], ed. S. Munk and Y.

Yoel, Jerusalem, 1931; Eng. trans. S. Pines, Chicago: University of Chicago Press, 1963.

——, *Letters* [*Iggerot ha-Rambam*], 2 vols., ed. Y. Sheilat, Ma'aleh Adumim: Ma'aliyot, 1988–89.

Marcuse, Herbert, "Repressive Tolerance," in *A Critique of Pure Tolerance*, ed. R. P. Wolff, B. Moore, and H. Marcuse, Boston: Beacon, 1969, 95–137.

Martin, Richard and Mark Woodward, *Defenders of Reason in Islam—Mu'tazilism from Medieval School to Modern Symbol*, Oxford: One World, 1998.

Maxwell, John, *Slavery and the Catholic Church: The History of Catholic Teaching Concerning the Moral Legitimacy of the Institution of Slavery*, Chichester: Barry Rose, 1975.

Menn, Stephen, "The *Discourse on the Method* and the Tradition of Intellectual Autobiography," in *Hellenistic and Early Modern Philosophy*, ed. J. Miller and B. Inwood, Cambridge: Cambridge University Press, 2003, 141–91.

Mill, John Stuart, *On Liberty*, ed. J. Gray, Oxford: Oxford University Press, 1991.

Nietzsche, Friedrich, *The Anti-Christ* [*Der Anti-Christ*] in *Twilight of the Idols and The Antichrist*, Eng. trans. R. J. Hollingdale, Harmondsworth: Penguin, 1968.

——, *Daybreak: Reflections on Moral Prejudices* [*Morgenröte. Gedanken über die moralischen Vorurteile*], Eng. trans. R. J. Hollingdale, Cambridge: Cambridge University Press, 1982.

——, *The Gay Science* [*Die Fröhliche Wissenschaft*], Eng. trans. Walter Kaufmann, New York: Vintage, 1974.

——, *On the Genealogy of Morals: A Polemic* [*Zur Genealogie der Moral: Eine Streitschrift*], in *On the Genealogy of Morals and Ecce Homo*, Eng. trans. Walter Kaufmann and R. J. Hollingdale, New York: Vintage, 1969.

——, *Werke: Kritische Gesamtausgabe*, ed. G. Colli and M. Montinari, Berlin: de Gruyter, 1967–84.

Noor, Farish A., Interview with Abu Bakar Bashir on *Aljazeera International*, 21 August 2006.

Nussbaum, Martha, *Cultivating Humanity: A Classical Defense of Reform in Liberal Education*, Cambridge, MA: Harvard University Press, 1997.

——, "Non-relative Virtues: An Aristotelian Approach," in *The Quality of Life*, ed. M. Nussbaum and A. Sen, Oxford: Oxford University Press, 1993, 242–69.

Nusseibeh, Sari, "What Next?" *Haaretz*, Eng. ed., 24 September 2001.

——, *What Is a Palestinian State Worth?* Cambridge, MA: Harvard University Press, 2012.

Nusseibeh, Sari and Ami Ayalon, "The Nusseibeh-Ayalon Agreement," *Haaretz*, Eng. ed., 3 September 2002.

Nusseibeh, Sari with Anthony David, *Once Upon a Country: A Palestinian Life*, New York: Farrar, Straus and Giroux, 2007.

Origen, *Against Celsus* [*Contra Celsum*], Eng. trans. H. Chadwick, Cambridge: Cambridge University Press, 1965.

——, *On First Principles* [*Peri archôn*], ed. and German trans. H. Görgemanns and H. Karpp, Darmstadt: Wissenschaftliche Buchgesellschaft, 1985; Eng. trans. G.W. Butterworth, New York: Harper and Row, 1966.

Oz, Amos, *A Tale of Love and Darkness*, Eng. trans. Nicholas de Lange, San Diego: Harcourt, 2005.

Parker, Arthur C., *The Constitution of the Five Nations*, Albany: University of the State of New York, 1916.

Pasquaretta, Paul, "On the 'Indianness' of Bingo: Gambling and the Native American Community," *Critical Inquiry* 20 (1994), 694–714.

Pines, Shlomo, "Outline of *A History of Arabic and Jewish Mediaeval Philosophy*," 1959, in C. Fraenkel, "Zur Integration von islamischem und jüdischem Denken: Eine unbekannte Projektbeschreibung von Shlomo Pines," *Münchener Beiträge zur Jüdischen Geschichte und Kultur* 2 (2008), 23–31.

Plato, *Platonis Opera*, ed. J. Burnet, Oxford: Oxford University Press, 1900–1907; Eng. trans. in *Plato: Complete Works*, ed. J. M. Cooper, Indianapolis: Hackett, 1997.

Popper, Karl, "Toleration and Intellectual Responsibility," in *On Toleration*, ed. S. Mendus and D. Edwards, Oxford: Oxford University Press, 1987, 17–35.

Rawls, John, *A Theory of Justice*, 3rd rev. ed., Cambridge, MA: Harvard University Press, 1999.

Raz, Joseph, *The Morality of Freedom*, Oxford: Oxford University Press, 1986.

Ricoeur, Paul, *Freud and Philosophy: An Essay in Interpretation* [*De l'interprétation: Essai sur Sigmund Freud*], Paris: Éditions du Seuil, 1965; Eng. trans. D. Savage, New Haven: Yale University Press, 1970.

Said, Edward, *Orientalism*, New York: Random House, 1978.

Sakai, Minako and Amelia Fauzia, "Islamic Orientations in Contemporary Indonesia: Islamism on the Rise?," *Asian Ethnicity* 15 (2014), 41–61.

Sartre, Jean-Paul, *La Nausée*, Paris: Gallimard, 1938; Eng. trans. R.

Baldick in *Nausea, or The Diary of Antoine Roquentin*, Middlesex: Penguin, 1965.
Sen, Amartya, *The Argumentative Indian*, New York: Farrar, Straus and Giroux, 2005.
Sextus Empiricus, *Outlines of Pyrrhonism*, in *Sextus Empiricus, Outlines of Scepticism*, ed. and Eng. trans. J. Annas and J. Barnes, Cambridge: Cambridge University Press, 2000.
Smith, James, *An Account of the Remarkable Occurrences in the Life and Travels of Col. James Smith during His Captivity with the Indians*, Cincinnati: Robert Clarke, 1870.
Spinoza, Benedictus de, *Ethics*, Eng. trans. E. Curley in *The Collected Works of Spinoza*, vol. 1, Princeton: Princeton University Press, 1985.
——, *Opera*, ed. Carl Gebhardt, 4 vols., Heidelberg: Carl Winters Universitätsbuchhandlung, 1925.
——, *Theological-Political Treatise*, Eng. trans. S. Shirley, Indianapolis: Hackett, 1998.
Stroumsa, Sarah, *Freethinkers of Medieval Islam: Ibn al-Rawāndī, Abū Bakr al-Rāzī and Their Impact on Islamic Thought*, Leiden: Brill, 1999.
Tarbell, Alice and Mary Arquette, "Akwesasne: A Native-American Community's Resistance to Cultural and Environmental Damage," in *Reclaiming the Politics of Health: Environmental Debate in a Toxic Culture*, ed. Richard Hofrichter, Cambridge, MA: MIT Press, 2000, 93–112.
Taylor, Charles, *The Ethics of Authenticity*, Cambridge, MA: Cambridge University Press, 1992.
——, "The Politics of Recognition," in *Multiculturalism: Examining the Politics of Recognition*, ed. A. Gutmann, Princeton: Princeton University Press, 1994, 27–73.
——, *Sources of the Self: The Making of the Modern Identity*, Cambridge, MA: Harvard University Press, 1989.
Tobias, John L., "Civilization, Protection, Assimilation: An Outline of Canada's Indian Policy," in *Sweet Promises: A Reader on Indian-White Relations in Canada*, ed. J. R. Miller, Toronto: University of Toronto Press, 1991, 127–44.
Turner, Dale, *This Is Not a Peace Pipe: Towards a Critical Indigenous Philosophy*, Toronto: University of Toronto Press, 2006.
Vickers, Adrian, *A History of Modern Indonesia*, Cambridge: Cambridge University Press, 2005.
Williams, Bernard, *Morality: An Introduction to Ethics*, Cambridge: Cambridge University Press, 1972.

Wisnovsky, Robert, *Post-classical Arabic Philosophy, 1100–1900: Metaphysics between Logic and Theology*, Oxford: Oxford University Press, forthcoming.

Wong, David, *Moral Relativity*, Berkeley: University of California Press, 1984.

York, Geoffrey and Loreen Pindera, *People of the Pines: The Warriors and the Legacy of Oka*, Toronto: Little, Brown, 1991.

Zeitlin, Hillel, *Baruch Spinoza: Hayyav, Sefarav ve-shitato ha-filosofit*, Warsaw: Halter, 1900.

INDEX